MESSAGES
FROM BEYOND

JUDITH BEALS

BALBOA.
PRESS

A DIVISION OF HAY HOUSE

Balboa Press books may be ordered through booksellers or by contacting:

Balboa Press
A Division of Hay House
1663 Liberty Drive
Bloomington, IN 47403
www.balboapress.com
1 (877) 407-4847

Because of the dynamic nature of the Internet, any web addresses or links contained in this book may have changed since publication and may no longer be valid. The views expressed in this work are solely those of the author and do not necessarily reflect the views of the publisher, and the publisher hereby disclaims any responsibility for them.

The author of this book does not dispense medical advice or prescribe the use of any technique as a form of treatment for physical, emotional, or medical problems without the advice of a physician, either directly or indirectly. The intent of the author is only to offer information of a general nature to help you in your quest for emotional and spiritual well-being. In the event you use any of the information in this book for yourself, which is your constitutional right, the author and the publisher assume no responsibility for your actions.

Any people depicted in stock imagery provided by Getty Images are models, and such images are being used for illustrative purposes only.
Certain stock imagery © Getty Images.

Print information available on the last page.

ISBN: 978-1-9822-2762-3 (sc)
ISBN: 978-1-9822-2764-7 (hc)
ISBN: 978-1-9822-2763-0 (e)

Library of Congress Control Number: 2019906846

Balboa Press rev. date: 05/20/2019

CONTENTS

DEDICATION

To the four most powerful, spiritual, amazing women who preceded, walk beside and extend the future for me.

My grandmother, Theresa Cote Gamlin, who inspired me from an early age.

My mother, Marie Sadie Boulanger, who was (and still is!) always there for me.

My niece and friend, Debee Boulanger, who spurred me on to share these messages

My granddaughter, Kristen Evans, who is a fantastic artist and "old soul."

INTRODUCTION

Life is very strange indeed. As children and young adults we make all sorts of plans and step forward into life only to find life is constantly changing and is not always what it appears to be. Often we "do it on our own" only to fall flat on our faces. As we mature, we begin to see that we need others, especially God. Some of us know Him from an early age, but others of us struggle to find something tangible that will allow us to "see" what life is all about. We get bogged down making a living, working out relationships, raising children, and striving for externals (things!) only to find we've come to a seeming dead end and get lost in a maze so complicated we can't find our way out. When we hit rock bottom, we are usually in such a vulnerable position that we can only look up, and that is often when our loving God reaches down to set us upright on our feet again. I know because I lived that life.

When I was very young, I knew God intimately and realized I had lived many times before. As an infant I remember thinking, *Why can't I control my hands?* I recall lying on a table and seeing light streaming through a nearby window.

Church was a terrible bore, and I sensed that money exchange was a large part of this ceremony. I grew up in a New England French family, so I heard the priest constantly speak of *d'argent*––money. They not only passed a basket, but a man went from row to row to collect seat money. I always thought that very strange and equated it with attending movies with my dad. Was this another show, an illusion?

I soon turned off the sermons because I saw through what was going on. I don't ever remember hearing about the love of God. I did love the crèche at Christmas and knew the Christ child was very special. I saw Christ as an adult hanging from the cross, but never did I realize how great God's love was for us.

At the tender age of five I was sent to parochial school, but it was so harsh and the nuns so strict and unloving, I decided to check out of the environment. I took ill and was sent to live with my grandmother, who lovingly cared for my open sores. (I had impetigo, which was highly contagious at the time and very difficult to cure as we had no penicillin or antibiotics.) Grandma Gamlin was a very spiritual person who had suffered much in life and had truly come to know God. She prayed for everyone and everything and set an example for me that I never forgot.

She had a picture above the bed of the Sacred Heart of Jesus, with a cross rising from the top of the heart and thorns surrounding it, as well. This picture captivated my attention frequently as it was fascinating and strange. She tried to explain what it meant because I questioned it, but the mystery of it all still eluded me.

Grandma read stories to me from a small, colorful book picturing the child, Jesus, as a young boy working with his carpenter father, Joseph. He was fashioning a small cross, and even now when I close my eyes, I can see those pictures of Jesus. My grandmother instructed me about the love that Christ gave to us and ultimately God, the Father, gave to us through His Son and the Holy Spirit (we called the "Holy Ghost"), for that was part of my blessed lessons taught by my beloved grandmother.

And so life moved on, and it was a happy, pleasant childhood with lots of love from family and friends. I romped in fields, chased after butterflies, and wondered at the big, fat spiders spinning their webs. I scraped my knees learning to ride a hand-me-down two-wheeler and fell from the rusty old gym set many times while learning to swing from it like a gymnast. I fished in the bullhead pond at twilight with my brothers and mother. The fish stung my hands more than once while removing the hooks from their mouths. It was such a joyous, fun-filled, happy time growing up that I was not prepared for the stark reality of an unhappy marriage in which I remained for nearly twenty-five years.

I raised three children and taught Junior High English, which was the happiest part of my twenties and thirties. But all this isolation, loneliness, and unhappiness began to catch up with me, and, as I had done in childhood, I became sick once again to set me aside from this unfulfilling, empty trap of an existence I had created for myself.

I ended up in bed for six weeks, and during that time I was given a book entitled *God Calling*. It was written by two women who meditated together each morning and wrote down the messages they received. I read it from cover to cover, excited and thrilled that God cared enough about us to speak to us directly. I threw the book onto the bed where I lay and exclaimed, "I can do this!" aloud. And thus began a life long journey, which is shared with you on the pages of this book.

And now, in the following pages, you will be hearing not from me, but from on high, or is it just beyond the veil in another dimension, the Great Beyond? As often as I have read these messages, there is always more to learn, and my greatest wish is that you will find, hidden in the messages, gems of knowledge that will assist you, comfort you, and sustain you as you walk the path to freedom and toward the Shining One of Eternity, only to be consumed forever into the light.

Judith A. Beals

CHAPTER ONE

JOURNEY TO ENLIGHTENMENT

The desert flows with the wind swirling at times, calm at other times, but constantly shifting, being rearranged by the winds that blow the sands hither and yon. Many people are like this, for they come and go with whatever happens in their lives. If good fortune exists, they are high on the crest of a hill of sand, and when ill fortune comes, they swirl in concentric patterns or dip into the chasms, overcome by seeming disaster. When one allows the I am to lead and control one's life and affairs, it is so different, for a calm exists in the center of a windstorm. When one is buffeted by the grains of sand or the winds of life flowing about, the God Presence acknowledged and relied upon fixes one to a rock, not allowing the being of light to be tossed about by any adversity or misfortune, for these are known by the soul to be lessons and blessings of growth and change. A diamond in the rough must be ground down here, polished to emit a wondrous light, and sparkle forth for all to wonder at and enjoy. You, Dear Ones, are gemstones in the making. Allow your beloved I am Presence to guide you through the labyrinth of life safely that you will shine forth for all time, a treasure in the coffers of the King of Creation. Continue to gather together for your own edification and guidance as well as a sharing of joy to others as you pray for them, too. Pray for the world that more light will surround her and protect the individuals who recognize the light that flows through all and is in all. When the light is honored,

1

life flows peacefully, and all is in harmony. The more this happens in individuals––this power to recognize and honor all creation––the nearer the Earth comes to the Golden Age. Pray for the Earth, and harmony will be a reality. I am with you always. I am St. Germain.

Broken Arrow Trail––Sedona, Arizona

Birds sing, for they are happy, content in the knowledge that life is filled with wonder and security. To be in nature surrounded by the light that fills all within view––trees, rocks, sky, clouds, and insects. This is the way to rejuvenate one's soul and being. The wind carries its message of calmness while caressing one's body and spirit. To appreciate life is a gift, for not all see the beauty around them. It is easier to be wrapped up in worldly activities, for calmness is disconcerting to many, for they are not accustomed to communing with their souls. Worldly ways wear down one's energy, whereas being amidst the stillness of creation energizes and fills one with more clarity and vision.

The sun's energy also contributes to the renewal process, for its light reminds one of the I am, which is its source. Human batteries need recharging frequently. Sleep is the manner in which most are renewed, but from time to time it is necessary to seek solace in the center of trees, mountains, and earth. It is a form of grounding, which connects one to Mother Earth. The solidness of this experience continues for much longer than a night's rest, for the beauty is absorbed into the psyche and is not soon forgotten. It is a high form of meditation to be able to contemplate creation, thereby understanding the Creator just a bit more.

Nature portrays many moods. At times it is calm, like today. Other times it is stormy, lighting the sky with electric charges of lightning accompanied by claps of thunder. It is an exciting time but can be dangerous for all standing tall. During exciting times in one's life, there is also an element of danger, for events unfold in rapid fire, one after another. Keeping a clear mind and a connection to the Godhead allows calmness to make the right choices moving through the time with ease. That, Dear

Ones, is why you are wise to keep your connection to the I am, for then you rely not on your judgments alone, but on the leadings of the Spirit who dwells within.

Hold time aside to rest in the arms of Father/Mother-God, whether it be in your own room or out in the peace of the wilderness. Renewed by your touch with eternity, you are better equipped to move through life. Be still and come to know the God within, and you will walk proudly and quietly through the confusion of the world. I am St. Germain, your friend, guardian, and teacher.

Rolling hills spread before you, for your walk will be constantly forward. Sometimes the path will wind to circumvent a problem area, but it will soon straighten out and continue its true course back to whence you came. All creatures of destiny walk this same path, but not all make it to their goal. Concentrate on the I am within, and you will be comforted, encouraged, and upheld as you venture forth along the path to truth, light, and love. Angels surround you even now, for as a creation of God you are blessed. Angels guard you and this will be more obvious as time goes on.

You will feel their presence and, yea, see them, as well. This is a time of transition, a time of intensity, a time for glorious acts of unselfishness in helping your fellow travelers. Some will rise to their glory instantly, for life is precarious; is it not? To know the I am that dwells within allows one to love themselves and others. Self-realization comes to those who intently seek answers to questions of importance. There is no place for fear in a heart filled with knowing, for to know that God dwells within all and is in all—the flowing, living light, the "glue" of the universe—allows a peace, a calm, that passes all understanding. It is so deep and abiding that nothing can prevail against this true awakening, which propels one forward at such speed that others are baffled and sometimes envious, as well. Do not look back, but continue this journey you have undertaken, for truly it will lead you to places you never dreamed possible. All things are possible with God. Release all cares to Him, for therein lies your freedom. "Let go and let God," should be the motto for your life.

I am St. Germain, a co-conspirator in the battle for life. Continue on, Dear Ones, and I promise to help you reach your goal. "All things work for good for those who love God!"

Consoling others brings greater peace to self, as well. All your actions bring back the same. When you live in peace and harmony with all, it comes back to you tenfold. Calming your inner spirit through decreeing and meditation allows the same to surround you daily. Delving into negative thought or fear thoughts brings the same to your door. Push away these thoughts and concentrate instead on lofty thoughts, quiet thoughts, peaceful, loving thoughts, and you will find your days filled with harmony and love. Your goal daily should be to fill yourself with a touch of Heaven through your quiet time, and then see how easily your days will flow.

The deeper and wider a river is, the quieter is its flow. A little brook gurgles, tumbles over obstacles, and is noisy. A creek is even louder, for it is shallow and has many obstacles before it in its path to a wider stream. Watch a river of depth flow, and you will see what I mean. It moves calmly, carrying with it all that rests upon its waters. The deeper and wider you make your spiritual life, flowing deep into the Presence, the calmer and quieter will be your spirit, and you, too, will flow easily, carrying all who come into your presence, as well. Your journey as a river flowing in the Spirit is ultimately to arrive at the ocean, the true immensity of the I am, the Cosmos Presence that encompasses all. To be in the Spirit is to eventually be taken into the Spirit, consumed with love and light, the very essence of all.

Growing in the Spirit brings one to self-realization, a depth of knowing that encircles and includes all knowledge, all love, all peace. Ascension comes after self-realization, or a being can choose to remain on this plane unaffected by negative energy to assist others on their path to enlightenment. This choice is before you in time. By joining forces with the Ascended Masters, you can make this choice to be helpers to others. Ponder this in your hearts, for workers are needed. Allow God's penetrating light to fill your being, speeding up the process of growth. I am Arcturus, your friend and guardian to the light.

There are many different types of birds. Some are graceful and fly freely, soaring, and climbing, and floating on the breeze. Others are very tiny, and you barely notice them as they flit from flower to flower. So many are large and unable to fly because of their awkwardness, and often long, gangly legs will not allow them this pleasure. The Divine Creator chose variety to display His glory in so many wondrous creatures of the air.

He also created man to be diverse, as well. Each person is unique and has his/her own characteristics. Some are tall and others short, whereas many (too many in this day and age) are fat, while others are thin. Even fingerprints of each person are different, and this is an identifying trait. Most inherit their temperament and physical aspects from their parents, but sometimes one can look and act like a distant relative and seem very different from his/her parents and siblings. Uniqueness is the glory of God's creations. He has placed a desire in each heart and soul to return to Him someday after lessons are learned and realization occurs.

Enlightenment begins with the true appreciation that the I am dwells within all creatures, plants, and the terra about you. You are all brothers and sisters, and the commonality of all is the Divine Presence within each heart.

Struggles will always be, for in these events of daily life, lessons are learned, and growth is certain. This life plane is difficult, true, but many souls choose to dwell here in order to grow, quickly satisfying the demands of karma. There are many things about your past you cannot understand, but know this—all will be revealed to you between lives, and a plan for your growth will unfold before you. I am St. Germain.

Rivers run free, dancing in the sunlight, rushing through narrow places, flowing when it has a wider passage. Its movement is natural and beautiful to behold. At other times it can be a raging monster, plowing down everything in its path, swallowing up houses, animals, and people, and dragging all in its way with it. Mostly however it is at peace and moving with its current flowing forward to its ultimate goal, unity with the ocean, the great sponge for itself.

And so, Dear Ones, you, too, are flowing like the mighty river, constantly moving toward the great light of God, from which you came. You, too, can rage and flow out of bounds without direction or purpose. When you are in sync with the Presence, you flow easily, and all around you benefit from the peaceful, calm flow of yourself and your life. To be moving toward your goal, it is essential to call forth the assistance of your I am Presence to help you move easily through life. Consider yourself a mighty river, a current of life flowing in a tranquil pattern back to your source. I am St. Germain, encouraging you this day, assuring you that we, the Ascended Masters, assist you in your journey back to your Creator-God.

The beauty of the Earth is as a balm to one's soul. Breathe deeply of the air; soak up the magnificence, for in it you will find peace, solace, and healing. The Earth's beauty is a reflection of the Almighty One of Heaven. Whenever you see, really see, the wonders of creation, you are in a state of meditation, for you are momentarily riveted to the radiance of colors and light, in fact the shimmering love of God presented to you in nature.

Go in peace this day clinging to the I am, the Creator, the Magnificent One of all Creation, the I am. I am St. Germain, protector of all light workers, ever present to lead and guide you one step deeper into God's plan.

Rubies, emeralds, diamonds, sapphires, and opals shimmer and shine, gleam and glitter in the sunlight, shining forth for all to see. Be in wonder, for the myriad colors of a handful of gems are radiant, healing, and magnificent to behold. All the gems in the world cannot match nor even approach the starry heavens, the towering mountains, the sparkling waters of the ocean, rivers, streams, and trickling brooks. The beauty of nature merely reflects the Almighty I am, and so when you view the wonders of nature about you, think on this fact: All creation of this planet is but a drop in the ocean of creation. Yet you stand in awe before a rainbow, or lightning, or a tumbling stream swollen with snow runoff. Remember that this is but one facet of the Creator-God.

If this truth can be absorbed, can you not realize that nothing is impossible to your Father-God? When you call to Him in desperation, will He not listen? He has given you a beautiful world, food to enjoy, and the love and companionship of others. Will He not carry this one step further and give you your heart's desires? The answer is there for you to grasp; is it not?

Ask and you *will* receive. Know this to be true, for your Father-God loves you as the most wonderful, amazing pinnacle of all creation, for you are made in His image, and you are reflections of the I am. In time you will be a blazing part of His radiance for you will ascend, rise into His own self. That day will be glorious, and then you, too, will shine forth forever, brighter, more opalescent, and more colorful than all the gems ever polished by man to radiate. You are being polished even now for every event, every test polishes you more and more each and every day. The more you resist, the longer the time it will take, but know this: it will happen much sooner than you think.

I am Arcturus bidding you to follow in the steps of the Masters, one small step at a time. Never despair, for all that comes your way is part of the Divine Plan.

The trees and plants in nature coexist with the forces of nature around them, which cause them to sway, be cold or hot, not have enough or too much water, or whatever comes to them. Yet they are able to ground themselves deep in the Earth and stay nourished and alive. Your grounding is in the I am, for that is what will enable you to come through life unscathed and unharmed. We are with you this day in all ways and will ever encourage you to walk forward one step at a time. Holiness is not an easy walk, nor have you ever been told it would be easy. Those around you who seem so together have the same doubts and fears that you do. Perhaps they're better actors, and in some cases they are truly happy in their roles, which come from knowing themselves in relation to the totality of life. This is what you are to strive for . . . a knowledge of what you as a created child of God mean in the total plan. You bring happiness to yourselves by accepting your place in life and blooming right where you are. We send you our blessings this day. I am Arcturus.

The beautiful sunrise each morning gives promise of a bright, multifaceted day in which there is a possibility of new heights that may be reached as the sun climbs the sky. As you move through the day, everything becomes clearer, and the realities of life open before you. Then it is up to you how you deal with the day's problems and occurrences. You can grow and evolve through the manner in which you meet these challenges, or you can digress because the opportunities are not grasped and met head-on, allowing lessons to be learned that growth might occur. The great gift of free will allows you choices, and you are masters of your destiny, and each outcome is a result of your choices. There are no accidents, Dear Ones, for you set yourselves up for what comes to you. Your mind controls whether you are happy, prosperous, and growing daily, or whether you are overwhelmed by others and the happenings you encounter. You can live happy, productive lives, or you can be in need and want. It is all up to you, for this life is an illusion that you create and control by your thoughts and feelings.

The transition of life unfolds before you slowly, and soon you are nearing the sunset time of your day on Earth, the planet where you can grow so rapidly that you are able to advance to new horizons, bringing you closer to your goal to live in sunshine always. The I am leads you to the vantage point where you can view the sunset of your life on this plane. The colors are transformed rapidly, and the myriad magnificence unfolds before you like a graceful dance of blending hues, some bright, some soft as they flow together. You are caught up in the rapture of the beautiful colors as the sun descends and night approaches. This is a time of rest for your soul that you might prepare for a new day in the cycle of life. I am White Buffalo Woman encouraging you to grasp the opportunities in your lives that you might join us in worshiping and giving honor to the I am within you.

A sunset of brilliant colors; pinks, oranges, reds, violets, and yellows, thrills the soul of the viewer, and yet this beauty would be there even if there was no one to appreciate it. And so, Dear Ones, your Father-God is always there in His brilliance and magnificence even if His creations do not honor Him. When you awaken to the wonder of your I am Presence, you then are able to appreciate the beauty that is all around you. So many meander through life like zombies, not even aware of the wonders of creation that abound on this Earth.

Your task is to awaken people to the truth that God dwells within, and when that is accepted and appreciated, then can those awakened begin to come alive to all that the Earth contains, for truly even the minute creatures and flowers contain a loveliness that no man can create. Artists awaken easily, for they are in tune by choice, for observation allows them to replicate that which they see. Falling short, they continue to create, for it is a consuming desire to reproduce some of the beauty around them. When artists create disharmony and ugliness, it is because their souls are not awake to the I am. It is essential for artists to tune into themselves first, and then can they give to the world the beauty to which others will respond. That is not to say that they must give exact replicas of what they see about them, but to give an interpretation of the art produced that will strike a cord deep in the viewer. Responding to nature and the wonders of other beings and creatures, the artist is a co-creator with the I am. Intensity of feeling is then expressed in a manner in which a work of art is given to the world in a way only that artist can give. We are, each one, co-creators, for we give to the life of others something unique, for we are responding to that which we see and feel. Open your eyes and hearts, for in receiving then can you give in a more perfect way. I am Arcturus, your friend and teacher.

Caramel-colored waves of wheat flow with the breezes, causing ripples to come one after another. The beauty of a huge field of wheat ripe and ready for the harvest is not unlike the field of beings before you who are also ripe for the Word of God, that He indeed dwells within each person. This revelation will cause ripples and waves to flow among the people, a pleasing sight to God the Father. You will help with the harvest through your prayers and decrees, for the field before you will shine with the brightness of the light that fills those ready to hear. Enlightenment is truly that, for a bright light of the I am begins to fill a soul open to the message of hope and true salvation from the denseness of this world. The more people who awaken, the less dense will be an area until the light obliterates the darkness.

A calmness settles in a place where children of the light congregate, and soon that peace spreads and brings all who are near into this paradise on Earth. It is like a sanctuary, a huge cathedral therein. Picture this multiplied by the thousands, for this is possible, Dear Ones, for the light travels very fast and touches each one with its radiant rays, sunbeams that light on each face, each heart, and each soul in its path. Some call it grace that pours down upon mankind, and that is very true. Some may reject this grace. Others will bask in it and be healed and whole once again like a little baby newly arrived from the beyond.

Wholeness brings enlightenment, and soon many, many souls will be renewed. You have no idea how powerful are your prayers and decrees. Trust what I say, for you are asked to continually pray for America and its inhabitants, for your friends and enemies, for your family and loved ones that all may truly walk upright touched by the light, filled with renewed hope, health, and well-being. I am Arcturus encouraging you forward in your endeavors.

CHAPTER TWO

WALKING IN THE LIGHT

Crystal mountains rise before you, drawing you ever deeper onto the path leading to a glory land of light shimmering in the distance. Look straight ahead, never veering from the way, for the rewards of a life in God's divine plan is far more satisfying and rewarding than any endeavor of a worldly nature. It reaches down into the deep recesses of your heart and soul, pouring a pure balm of energy and brightness that obliterates the high noon sun in summer. It is a light that does not harm your eyes, but soothes the very longings of your soul and heart. In His kingdom are many paths, many destinations, and many callings. To view the entire plan is impossible, but to walk the path of righteousness is to comfort and placate all your longings, for it is the correct choice for you each individually. You cannot walk another's path. You can parallel another's, but your calling is unique, and always you are led by your angels and guides down a path overshadowed by protective trees of life-giving shade that encompass your life and lead you safely to your destination. Hovering always nearby are beings of light who rejoice when you return to the path after wandering or, more importantly, reach your high points after struggle to rest and renew strength to forge onward again.

Life is a labyrinth complete with circuitous paths, dead ends, and straight parts that flow easily and happily along like a large, gently flowing river. Other times you face rapids swirling dangerously about you. Remember at these times to go within for assistance, for therein dwells your I am ever ready to come to your defense with insights that assist you in flowing past the danger of destruction. You cannot be destroyed, Dear Ones, for you are protected at all times by angels.

Do not think that any happening, good or bad in your eyes, is happenstance for it is put before you to assist you in your growth to allow the next portion of the path to rise before you, drawing you ever nearer to the goal of life everlasting in the arms of the Sacred One of Eternity. How blessed you are when adversity comes before you, for it offers you another opportunity for growth unparalleled by any design you could concoct, for when you ride out the seeming problem, you will find it was perfect for you to change what needed to change or correct that which needed correction. Learn to embrace life in all its aspects for resting with the flow, the ebb, and tide of living, will allow the happiness you seek, for joy and happiness begin in your heart, Dear Ones.

A heart filled with gratitude for the little gifts of life will surely be overjoyed when the grand gifts of good fortune come your way. Do you want to continue giving gifts to one who barely recognizes them? Of course not. So then does it not continue that gratitude for gifts that flow to you from on high will please your Father/Mother-God who will shower more and more upon you? Test this and see if it is not truth that I, St. Germain, speak. Hold fast to the way, and blessings will fall upon you in a steady stream, tumbling down like a waterfall. Oh, how blessed you are, Dear Children of the Light. We stand beside you even now ready to assist you, comfort you, and show you the way to eternity.

Circles flow around you when you are balanced. They represent unity with the I am. They are never ending, flowing easily and smoothly. Circles are fascinating to many artists, and you see them much in artwork. Man is constantly striving for perfection in all about him, often ignoring the fact that perfection is actually within. Energy centers of the body are called chakras. They are actually flowing circles of energy when in balance, allowing the person to function well in his physical, emotional, psychic, and spiritual life. In fact, that is life––to be flowing smoothly in one's body and soul. Good health is from this flow of energy, for when chakras are blocked and not flowing in concentric circles of energy, those areas are stagnated, and disease sets in. This is how tumors develop in one's body. It is well to visualize the circles of energy flowing in all the chakras, for if they are not flowing properly, it will stimulate them to flow. All life is intended to flow in circular energy patterns, looking very much like spirals. The whole universe flows in this manner according to divine plan. Each person is like a little universe. The hum or "ohm" of life flows like a wonderful machine. When you are balanced and in tune with the I am, your life will also flow quietly, peacefully, and smoothly, emitting the ohm sound that is life.

Once again we ask you to visualize this flow of energy about and within you, for then you are in tune and receptive to guidance from the I am that your days will be in harmony with all life teeming about you. Those of like mind will be drawn into your presence, and the energy created will be brighter than the sun at noonday. I am St. Germain instructing you this day. How happy we are when you are in tune walking in the light.

I am using all things to grow you up. Your care and welfare are My Concerns. Others are wrapped up in their own problems. I am wrapped up in you. I am God and creator of your soul. A creator loves His creation, for it is for His glory. I delight in you. I honor your attempts to come to me. Though you stumble, I will reach down to lift you and set you on course again. You are always so anxious to get somewhere; you don't even know where. Relax, calm down——be patient so that I may guide your progress. Put one foot before the other and trust that I am there to uphold you. You try to run before you know how to walk. Stop and think before you continue. Grasp My Hand if you feel you are about to fall. I am always by your side, steadying you as you totter in My Will. I am not discouraged by your faltering steps or even when you fall. Why do you get discouraged with your failings? Just turn to me immediately, and I will put you back on the path with loving arms, reaching out to uphold you momentarily until you can stand and walk again. You know how your own children learned how to walk. So it is with you now. You are learning how to walk in the kingdom of God. All new beginnings are difficult, but get easier as you learn little lessons firsthand as they are needed. Do not be discouraged, Child. I am with you, and I love you in spite of your failings and weaknesses. I know what they are as I see the heart I created, but I see so much more good in your heart. You desire to do My Will, and I see that most clearly. Your Creator and Father-God.

Always keep in mind that you are a child of God and as such can expect the good that comes from your Father in Heaven and in your heart. It is so difficult for Earth children to understand that God lives within and without, as well, but He/She does. You have your being in Him, and you have all the life around you, animate and inanimate, filled with the light of God. It is humans who bring in the darkness and dwell upon it. That is what causes discord, for the natural state of existence is truly in peace, light, joy, and happiness. Look at the creatures around you, the birds, the little and big animals, as they trust the Creator and approach life that way. They do not fret or worry. They do not dwell in negativity. They sing, they spin, they play, and they rejoice in life. Take lessons from them, and you, too, will begin to be joyous, at peace, and in abundance, for you will appreciate every minute of your life and rejoice in it by spreading your love and joy to others around you. That, my Dear Ones, is the meaning of life––to learn to trust, to learn to love innocently with no thought of return, to learn to take joy in your very existence, and to spread that joy to others. Life is and can be easy if you just relax and allow it to flow as a river from its source to its destination. The goal of life should be to return to your source, God, from whom all good things flow. Keep your eyes on the light, and do not divert from it. I want you all to come to this realization so that externals do not interfere with the path you have chosen. I am St. Germain, your teacher and friend.

I will guide each step as you move about in My Will. I will *not* bless your attempts to go ahead of My Time Schedule. You still have vestiges of impatience in your being. You are a doer, and this is why I will use you, for

I know you will perform the tasks I have laid before you. But you must learn to listen to My Voice and follow the urgings of My Spirit. I will lead you into areas I've planned in order to complete, begin, or continue the work I plan––My plan, not your plan. Do not be upset if My Way doesn't always make sense, for the goal is not always reached by a direct course, but often a circuitous, mazelike course is more beneficial to accomplish the task.

Rest in me, Child, for I am using you here as I will use you everywhere and in every circumstance. How pleased I am when you truly give me free reign, for then I can pour blessings upon you and yours in a steady downpour. When you don't yield your life to me, only a sprinkling of My Graces patter down upon the parched, arid existence you are enduring. I haven't called you to merely endure. I've called you to overcome and to walk upright in the glory of My Light. You are called to be children of light, and that light is me shining in, around, and through you. That is what it means to be children of light.

Bees can sting and thereby cause pain to the recipient of the bite, but they make honey, as well, which is sweet and tasty to the one who partakes of it. This brings great joy and pleasure to mankind. You, too, Dear Ones, can bring pain or joy to others, depending upon your mental attitude. It is your free choice to spread joy or to bring pain to others. When you remain conscious of the I am, you can fill your being with light, love, and joy, and these in turn are passed onto those you encounter each day. Spread God's joy, and you, Dear Children of the Light, will also be filled with joy beyond anything you can imagine. Be in peace this day, and walk in the light that surrounds you. We are with you, guiding you and surrounding you with peace and protection. I am St. Germain, your mentor and guardian.

Enfold these mysteries within your hearts, for I wish to enlighten you this day. I am St. Germain, your teacher and proponent. When you deal with your fellow man, always stay in the power of the I am Presence. All you need do is concentrate on the I am, knowing that He dwells within thy heart, and allow His thoughts to fill your mind and then speak forth, knowing His power is in action and His truth is coming out of your mind from your heart. It is important that you speak out in your defense with a lilting song of light and love, for darkness must flee before the brilliant light of the I am. Try this and see if it is not true, for by speaking forth truth, you set in motion solutions to your problems. You are not bound by the Earth's ways. You dwell in the light of the I am, and you speak in His name. Always be mindful of His presence within, relate through Him to Him in others, and you will be victorious.

Juggling the busy aspects of your life, sometimes you forget that God is in charge, for you have given Him this honor. Stop and allow Him the opportunity to work out the details. Tune into Him daily for guidance preferably in the beginning of your day. Listen and allow your heart to direct you as you prepare for the day's activities. You will find life moves much more smoothly, and blessings will touch you and those around you, as well, for the offshoot of God's love living in you flows out to others also.

Punctuality of timing will astound you, for each part of the puzzle will fall easily into place. His perfect timing far exceeds our plotting, planning, and fretting. Let go and know all is well and moving forward with ease as long as you submit the problems to Him. Expect answers and they will come. Expect supply and it will come. Expect miracles and they will certainly be before you. You are children of the Almighty. Do not hesitate to claim your kinship with the I am. Your lives will be miracles to you and wonders to those around you. Have faith in the goodness of the I am Presence, trusting your life will be a shining example of trust and abundance.

I am St. Germain and have come to you to remind you to let go and let God work in and for you

Glorious is the heavenly host who sing praises to the Mighty I am constantly, for He alone is worthy of this praise. And so, Dear Children of

the Light, sing His praises as often as you can, for it uplifts you and raises your consciousness from the pettiness and negativity of the world, which dwells in such and concerns itself with naught but this. You are called away from this, for it does not fit you any longer. Dwell in the world, Dear Ones, for that is where you've been placed, but do not be of the world and be concerned by negative thoughts, feelings, and desires. Be above this, for in your residing in the light, you will see these things fall away, and in its place will be the essentials of love, light, understanding, and acceptance of all that is around you and all those you meet along life's way.

Duplicity is not for you, for it will tear at you and bring you down. Stay focused on the I am, and all this will fall away, and you will be in peace filled with joy, happiness, and the love of the I am.

Daily you are growing, and your hearts are becoming purer, for the Violet Flame is in fact the power of God as it flows through you, cleansing, healing, and purifying you. The Divine cannot dwell in a body and soul that is not being purified by the Presence.

Oh, how wondrous is the way of our I am Presence! You will see more clearly as the days move by. I am Arcturus, and I will protect and defend you this day. Go in peace and find joy.

The clouds about you are puffy, white, and luminous now. They stand before and around you as reminders of the varied beauty of the heavenly hosts who protect your being. Absorb them into your soul as you view them, and know that the light of the I am is one thousand times brighter and more opalescent, always shining forth, lighting your path to total freedom. You are blessed, Dear Ones, and your days will be filled with such happiness that you will rejoice always that the I am has revealed gems of truth to you that you never understood before. Each day will be filled with learning and enlightenment, for your teacher dwells within your heart. I am Arcturus and wish you peace and love this day.

Love is the key that opens every door to every storehouse in the universe. Filling your heart with the love of the I am through opening to it and the decrees (prayers) you say enable you to surround yourself with all good that protects you, defends you, surrounds you, and brings you into a place of joy and happiness. Feel the love in your heart, for it is joy and happiness. Feel the love in your heart, for it is the manifestation of the Presence confirming that you are in the arms of the I am, and His light surrounds you. Nothing can penetrate this light, for it acts as a shield that is impenetrable. You walk with protection about you. Evil is repelled by this and will not touch you unless you allow access to your being. Holiness comes from the I am and floods your being and soul so that each day you bring this light with you, and it flows to others you meet. The strength of the I am fills you, and you command each situation in a loving manner so that others will respond to the God Presence within you.

Comfort is always there for you, for when you reach out, it will immediately encircle you and make you secure. Tears purify the soul and allow healing to penetrate the deep niches of your heart. It is a gift that enables humans to renew themselves and let go of deep-seated emotions that cause harm to the body and psyche when stored and locked away. Emotions released and felt give solace and reduce stress, which debilitates one and reduces one to a victim of the world's ways.

You are not of the world. Do not allow the petty problems of yourself or those around you to encumber you, for that is not for you to deal with or worry about. Instead hand these problems over to the I am and watch miracles occur, for He will reduce these problems to a dot, and then they will disappear. I am Arcturus and wish you well this day. Open to the leadings of the I am, and He will guide you in all you do.

The stars in the heaven shine brightly at all times even though clouds often obliterate their glow. How much more is our constant love for you, Dear Child of Destiny? How often in the past you have fallen to your knees, literally and figuratively. We uplifted you and set you on course again that you will be drawn more closely to your goal, life in the light always and forever.

The time is coming when all men will see the light, for events will occur to draw mankind back into the fold and back onto the path. How much I love you all! I have breathed life into you, setting your hearts afire with the steady beat that pulses until the silver cord is severed, and your spirit returns to me. Life is a wondrous gift, Child, and I desire all to honor the giver of gifts, for I love my created children with an everlasting, magnificent outpouring of pure love. This love I pour onto you must be shared and spread to all you meet each and every day, for that is the glue that holds all together. If you could see the light that flows through all, including the inanimate, you would fall on your knees in honor and praise of me, for it is overwhelmingly beautiful, this love. Go now and live this day in love. I am that I am.

Nothing or no one is static. All life changes constantly, and this concept is to be part of your conscious mind. Each and every person is constantly growing, for each experience contributes to change. Do not stereotype anyone or anything, but be willing to realize and accept the fact that everything is in flux, and all life is moving at all times. I will take this one step further for you, Dear Ones. Do not allow others to treat you as though you have not changed. You can do this in a loving way, but stand straight, and in love show the change and growth you have experienced. Families are often the least accepting of your change. Once again in a loving way, show them you have changed, always remembering that they too have undergone growth and change.

Stay in the light, love all with whom you interact, and you will find true happiness and joy as an added bonus. I am St. Germain requesting that you follow this more perfect way of living your life. You will never feel turmoil again if you can follow this basic plan for living.

A tie is a useless object that man wears because he thinks it adds to his appearance. We hold onto many useless objects and imperfections in our lives, not because we feel they enhance us, but because we cannot let go of them. When we come to the realization that they are indeed bogging us down, we, with the help of the I am, can let them go and be much lighter and happier as a result. When you recognize the lack of need for these imperfections and allow the Violet Flame to dissolve them, you will be much happier and less entangled in worldly ways. You are not of this world, but are much lighter beings placed here to eradicate the minor (and sometimes major) flaws in your being that must be eliminated in order for you to come into a fuller life filled with the Divine.

Let me explain what it means to be a child of the light. You, over many, many lifetimes, have come to a point where you are more spiritually inclined than worldly. You seek the light more fully because you are more comfortable in the light than in pursuing the world's ways, which seem gray and dim in comparison. You are compelled by your progression to want and need more knowledge of the I am's ways because you prefer the light to the darkness of Earth. When you gain more insight and awareness, you come ever nearer to desiring to be in the light all the time. Having come to this point, you are more accepting of others and all that happens around you. You have arrived at the realization that your life is in control of the I am, and this is important––because you have placed it there willingly. Rest in the knowledge that all good will comes from this surrender, and your needs will be met here and eventually beyond. I am Arcturus and bid you greetings and love from the Ascended Masters.

Infinity is not a number, for the two are not compatible. Infinity is unlimited, going on forever, never ending nor passing from existence. God is infinity, and so is all energy, for it merely passes into a new state again, and again, and again. You, Dear Ones, are also infinite, for you are part of the Divine. You have lived many, many lives, for always you are given opportunities to be taken ever deeper into the Almighty, reconnecting with the Presence who dwells in all. Once your mind accepts the fact that you contain the I am and are part of the Divine, you can reach out for assistance to your I am Presence and those who have attained their ascension, the Masters, who are ever ready to assist you to your ascension as well. We are all part of the One, all part of the whole. There is no division except that which we see as division. We create our own separation from others and, in so doing, exclude ourselves from life. When we seek unity, we find connection to others and our Creator, for it is true we are all one in One. We are infinite, for we are part of the Divine and will always be no matter how limiting we perceive life. Life, Dear Ones, goes on forever, for you are merely transformed into a new place, a new state of existence, where, as always, you are given more opportunities to learn, grow, and "see." All life is constantly in flux. Nothing ever stands still. Only your finite mind limits you, for you draw to yourself that which you perceive as truth. All that comes into your life has been drawn to you by your own thinking. You and only you limit your world. That is always open to change. You only have to erase yesterday's limiting thoughts to change them with today's expanding thoughts to create a new existence for yourself and those with whom you share this portion of your life.

Open your mind and heart, see the light that surrounds you, and be filled with this light that is Divine. Light flows through all persons, places, and things. When there is darkness, it is because of limiting thoughts in the minds of those who seek darkness rather than the light. Fear is often the reason people seek the dark, for they fear the light and therefore reject it. How sad it is. Enlightenment, Dear Ones, is merely walking back into the light, shedding fears and finding joy, happiness, contentment, warmth, and most of all love that comes from the light. Raise your arms and hearts to the light. Embrace it and be filled with it, for it is home, Dear Ones. Stepping into the light brings you back to your source, which is home to your soul. Rejoice and be glad, for no matter how many times you wander, it is wonderful to return to your source, your solace, your haven.

Be at peace this day, imbued with the knowledge that you are loved, honored, protected, and comforted by the Presence who is all in all, pure love——our Father/Mother-God. I am Arcturus with a message of hope and love to each one who calls to us and the Almighty One for assistance.

The clearing in a forest is a special sight for light streams down from above penetrating the dense vegetation allowing a special glow that is hard to duplicate any other way. Consider this spot a place for pause and meditation. Visualize it and enter the center of it in your mind's eye. It will bring peace and healing to your soul for it will be a special place in which to spend time communing with your soul wherein you will find your guides and your creator.

Visualize the soft light penetrating your being lighting you up from within and touching cords deep inside that set in motion a distinct hum or ohm – a sign of connection to Spirit for edification and healing.

When you visit this special place daily, you will begin to "see" things much differently for you are being filled with love that must be shared with all around you. How blessed you will be to be filled with the Divine which you can easily pass on to those you encounter. It is a far better way to start your day and, yes, to end it as well.

Sleep time is often a busy time for your soul for it is a time of learning, refreshing and solving the numerous problems of your life. Your subconscious is more open to God and thus, when your mind is quiet, you can receive precious help to enable you to continue life in this very dense environment. What a great plan from a wonderful Creator! Stay in the light and you will be renewed and healed. I am your friend, Arcturus.

This is a momentous day for all citizens of the world for Light from above is bathing the world bringing love and all good for everyone. Your Creator – God loves each person with an intensity that cannot be measured. He longs for his creations to return to the fold giving honor, praise and thanksgiving for life everlasting.

If you emulate Father/Mother God in your dealings with all you approach each day, you will emit naught but love, forgiveness and peace of spirit. It is the right way to live for it brings love, harmony and joy back to the sender. Remember that what you give out comes back to you tenfold. If you give out hate, it will return in an avalanche of dis-ease which can settle in your body but will definitely settle in your aura. When you send out love, it also comes back and fills your space with the same. Your aura will shine with sparkling lights as new-fallen snow in the moonlight.

Diamond-lights will fill your space and most will want to be near you to absorb the overflow.

Smile and be kind and you will be happy forever. Calm and peace will abound about you and all, including God's special gifts - animals, will be drawn to you as though you were a magnet.

Turn your faces to God and He/She will fill you to overflowing with His wondrous love and peace. It is time to receive directions from on high for the tasks before you are gigantic, overflowing their bounds. Do not feel insignificant or ineffective for it will not be you and you alone who will minister to the needs of the masses. We, the Ascended Masters, and all the Saints in heaven will fill you with their strength and guidance that comes from God, Himself.

When you apply for a job, there are many competitors and only a few will be chosen to compete for the final interview. You, dear ones, are among the final group and will move forward with others of like-mind to do the work set before you. I am St. Germain and I will lead you always.

Holiness is not learned over night nor is it learned without lessons that give insight into our weaknesses allowing us to address them and grow stronger. Over many, many lifetimes a soul develops and comes to a point wherein nirvana is reached. When this occurs a soul is so in tune with Mother/Father God he/she could walk on water or bi-locate if it is needed. Then that soul is what the church calls a saint. This means he/she is a direct conduit and God's energy and "miracles" abound to all around the "saint." Jesus reached this in one short life and was in direct connection with God. He is revered by many and rightfully so as the son of God. On the other side he works tirelessly assisting mankind who is struggling to connect to God. He is a wondrous interceder who works out of pure love.

I am Arcturus and wish to enlighten you as you traverse the pathway to your heavenly home. Workers are needed to protect the Earth and its inhabitants and you are called to assist us, the Ascended Masters, in that task. Workers are few and time is short until the Earth's people open their eyes and hearts to the glorious future that beckons them. The scale is tipping toward the side of righteousness, and mankind is struggling to take hold of Divinity and all it promises. Do not fret over this for it will come into being and all will rejoice deep within for the grace poured upon them. Those who reject this will be drawn to another place where they too will come to awakening in their own time. God does not overstep free will but gently calls and urges and sets forth circumstances to bring His created children back to Him/Her.

Rest assured you are coming closer to what you have been working for these many lives. Blessings to you this day and all the days of your life on Earth.

CHAPTER THREE

COME TO ME

"As far as the sky above the Earth are My Ways above your ways. You cannot see My Total Plan for all of you. Only trust me that it is a perfect plan from a perfect God. You are My Beloved, and I see your efforts to come to me and abide in me. I will strengthen you in your groping, and you will be blessed and rewarded."

You are being led by your Father in Heaven, for as you turn to Him more, He is there instantly, for He dwells within. He wishes to put good things upon His children, and as each one turns to Him, He responds with love and blessings.

It is thrilling to watch how He pours wonders and joys upon you, for you will feel His hand more in your life each day. You have no concept of how powerful these decrees are, and as you say them more and more, you will see miracles popping all around you like firecrackers on the Fourth of July. The brilliance of God's love is like the fireworks display, for the beauty is there, and we get glimpses of it, and then it appears to fade, but this is not so, for His love always shines brightly. We are the ones who don't always see it. The flashes we see from time to time keep us going and put us back on the path. I am St. Germain.

I wish to come to you today in a special way, for you are moving through and beyond a time when growth has been very dramatic and rapid. Your desires are being taken care of in ways beyond your expectations, for you see concentrating on me and My Presence within you opens doors to treasures not of this Earth, but where they really matter. Your being delights in these riches, for it has a built-in sensor that zeroes in on the treasures and riches of the deep soul seat, your central core of existence through all time, past and present, for, you see, you have always been a part of me even though you might have wandered away from me. A father or mother who truly loves his or her child will always wait patiently for the errant offspring to return and then shower love on him or her. And so it is, Dear One, with me, your heavenly Father. I wait patiently for you to return, and, in fact, I allow circumstances and people to come into your presence and cause you to return to me faster. It was necessary for you to move through the last year in order to allow the dross to rise to the top to be seen and removed. Fine steel is tempered this way in a caldron, and when the dross is removed, what remains is strong. You are now much stronger and capable of holding up yourself and others who will be sent your way. Whenever My Chosen Ones go through difficulties, it is to be used in the future to help others who need to see me more clearly.

I bless you and ask you to continue concentrating on me, your Lord and Savior and lover of your soul. I am that I am.

Come to me. Reside in My Presence at all times. Let My Spirit purify you in thought, word, and deed. Open yourself to the purifying work of My Spirit, who will lead you onto paths of righteousness. You call me Lord, so now let me *be* your Lord——Lord of your day and night, your happiness and your sorrow, your pain and your joy. Open every facet of your life to me that I might bless you while renewing and refreshing you.

I have your future in My Hands, as you have given me that privilege. You desire to give me your life, and so I have taken it and *will* use it in ways you cannot comprehend. I will lead you one step at a time. I go before you, clearing the path, preparing the way before each step you take. I will not let one pebble stay in the way, but will remove obstacles, big and little, before you that you may do the work I have set before you. You will use all the talents I have placed within your potential, and they are many——much greater than even you know. I see how I have made you. I see what stuff you are made of——and it *is* good. You are china, not pottery . . . *but* you are in the refining stage even now. You will be ready soon. The more you yield to My Polishing Process, the faster you will be ready to accomplish the chores I've set for you to do.

Humility and submission are the attributes I am fashioning into your being. Love that comes from me will burn them into your makeup until they are fused and welded into your being. Tempering is always a painful process, but you can speed up the process and allow it to be easier by relaxing and trusting me. I will not test you beyond your endurance or leave you half-finished. I will continue to mold and refine you until you are done.

Trust me, My Child, for it is in trusting that the pain will cease. I will only allow what is right for you to befall you, for I am the Master-Planner, the Creator of the Blueprint, and the Master-Builder, the Refiner, the Mason, the Carpenter. I am about a mighty work of fashioning, rebuilding what has been torn down. At some stage I may tear down more and then rebuild that area, as well. It is an ongoing process, but it is with patience and love that I fulfill My Plan for you. Join me in rejoicing as each brick is put in place. Your foundation will be solid, for it is I who will be the foundation of your life. Hold to me, and never let go. My Light will shine forth through you even as the building is being erected. Trust me.

Look to me now and always in all ways. Hold fast to the promise of everlasting life. This is a testing ground. Just as an airplane is tested while in its early stages, so are you being tested and refined. Adjustments are often made in the plane, and so must adjustments be made in you. You will be able to soar to new heights in My Spirit after they have been made. The biggest adjustment now is to follow My Leadings, placing me first, from which place I had slipped due to your desires and idol worship. Come into My Holy Presence once again. Remove your sandals, for you will tread on holy ground. I am calling you into My Presence to sanctify you for the future tasks I have set aside for you to perform. A deep infilling of My Spirit is needed to keep to My Plans and not deviate from My Way. Your humanness is not to be put down, as I created you to be human, but this humanness must be transformed into transparency that My Glory and Light may shine through. I need you to perform My Will, to be My Representative in a world of darkness and despair. My Victory is yours for the claiming. Come into My Presence for strength, comfort, direction, and an infilling of My Spirit. I will personally anoint you to do My Service.

Just as the tides of the sea wash ashore treasures from the depths, particularly after a storm, so it is when you allow waves of my gems of knowledge to wash up into your consciousness that you will find answers to your problems and woes.

Truth is a bright-colored conch that gleams in the sunlight, reflecting my rainbow and shining forth for all to see. Where truth is held in esteem, My Spirit abounds and has a place of honor.

The round sand-dollar treasures are discovered as you trod the wave-washed sands that encircle the ocean depths of my life, which is fathomless. I have given these treasures of knowledge into your keeping that you might share them with others who sorely need to hear that I am real, that I am in charge of all that happens, and that I allow changes in the tides of mankind in order to draw each being into My Luminous, Never-ending Presence. How happy I am when one of My Creations opens to My Love and seeks for Myself. It is a time when angels of light rejoice, for they are receiving a new member into their unending chorus, who chant my praises into eternity. All my creations were made to sing out praises unto me and rightfully so, for I alone am worthy.

The ocean is a reminder of My Flowing, Moving, Ever-Changing Life. That is why so many of My Children are drawn to the seashore for comfort and refreshment. Instinctively they know that the ever-rolling seas are mirrors of the vastness of their Creator, whose depths are immeasurable by mere humans. The treasures locked in the depths of the seas are much like the treasures man can find in me. I will dole out thoughts and revelations to man from the great Consciousness as needs arise. How often are men spurred on to pursue scientific knowledge, when all they need do is turn to me for the answer. I desire to share with My Creations knowledge as it is to assist men in easing the cares, woes, and difficulties of life. The keys to the treasure house are in the care of those who unlock the Consciousness by seeking me. I am who Am.

Humans are as I have made them––frail and weak. I have intended it this way that they may depend on me and me alone. Other humans are weak, so do not look to them for the strength you need to overcome the world. Come to me, My Child, and cling to me alone. I will strengthen and support you as I am the only foundation you can build on that endures.

People will pass in and out of your life, leaving you that which you need to strengthen, sustain, build you up, and, yes, even uproot parts of you that need to be removed. I am the only person in your life that is permanent because you are part of me. You are My Creation, My Glory on Earth, My Masterpiece. I see in you beauty that comes from me. I am not disappointed in you. Why are you disappointed in yourself?

I have called you to fulfill a purpose, and I will reveal My Plan step by step. I am leading you through an obstacle course to show you how to overcome through My Power, My Life that is in you. *Believe* that I am in you, and you will begin to comprehend your worth, your value. I am not corruptible flesh. I am Spirit! Those who let My Spirit lead will not be disappointed. Do you remember the Twenty-Third Psalm? I am the Shepherd for your soul, guiding and leading you back to My Father from whence you came. Rejoice in that! I am leading you to My Father through the divine workings of My Spirit, who is making you whole, and new, and lovelier––a gift for your Creator.

Look to me and not into a mirror of me––another person is what I mean. True, the beauty in others is from me, and to it you are drawn. I fill those closest to me with Myself, and that is what you are drawn to, more in some than others. When you are repulsed by some, it is because they are following their own ways and not My Ways. I cannot shine through them as I ought, so that is what turns you away from them.

Each face you encounter was created to shine with My Light and Love. Since darkness often pervades their being, My Light cannot shine through. They need to hear about me in order to turn to me. My Spirit is being poured out these days as never before. I *long* for My Dear Creations to come back to their Creator. It is as it was meant to be, but how few even know me . . .

CHAPTER FOUR

BEING A LIGHT TO OTHERS

The Golden Rule should be foremost in your dealing with others. No *one* is better or lesser than another. Do not criticize or be judgmental. Each person brings along their baggage, and it inhibits their relaxation ability and their trust abilities, as well. By being accepting and loving to all in your words *and* actions, each will respond to the God within you. *That* is what matters, Dear Ones, for you will be signposts to the I am. All men seek serenity and love. When they see it in you, they will be curious. Some will be ready to walk the same path. Others will not. The main thing to remember is that at least for a brief time, another saw God in you. It *will* make a difference even if it's a tiny step for his soul growth. Rome wasn't built in a day, and spiritual growth takes time, too. Not all are struck from their horse as St. Paul was, and yet miracles still do happen, and God still touches some in a mighty way. Rejoice that this is true.

As for you, Dear Ones, continue your journey and open your hearts that they may be cleansed more and more each day. Say the decrees and prayers for yourself and others. By praying for others, you're extending yourself in love. That is good, and know this: You can never give away love without receiving it back tenfold, for it comes back to you in waves and floods your mind and soul. I am your friend and guardian, St. Germain.

This is a new day to use for God's glory and your wellbeing. Open your eyes and see the beauty of the Earth about you. Open your ears and hear the sounds of the birds chirping in their happiness to be alive. Open your heart to receive love from your fellow humans, and be ready to give love, as well. When you are aware of the I am Presence, love just naturally bubbles up inside and flows out to others. Be at peace knowing all is well with your world, for you will attract good to yourself in many forms, including supply. Good health will you want to seek, for it will enable you to continue this path to enlightenment. Your body is your temple filled with the love that comes from the Presence within you, and when your body is not a pure vessel, it must be cleansed that more light can fill you and shine forth as a beacon to others in need. There are so many seeking the pure light that comes from the I am alone. Tinsel lights and worldly pursuits are empty, and so many trod that path to nowhere and are disillusioned, for they sense something more. All men seek that which is right inside, and they know it not. You, Dear Ones, are called to spread the Word about the light and new life you have found.

The intensity of your experience must be shared with others, for that is how God's kingdom on Earth is spread; example and testimony are what I refer to. You see, when example is missing, testimony is empty, and so, Dear Ones, you must live your life in peace, harmony, and love, for then you really need not speak, and others will know you are different. You are not called to be weak, but to stand strong in your convictions, and do not allow others to bowl you over. Stand straight and command the respect of others, for they will sense you cannot be overtaken by their worldly desires or selfishness. All good things will come to you when you are secure in your own self-knowing that you are a child of the universe, a special being infused with the love and essence of God, the I am. I am Arcturus encouraging you to strength and always to love.

Many changes are coming to Earth that will bring millions of people back to God. They will once again kneel and ask forgiveness and begin to worship once again. In times of peril each comes back to his/her foundation which is family and early memories of another land their DNA remembers.

The connection to God can never be severed for we live in God-substance and are indeed images of Him as He intended. We were created from His own substance and are imprinted forever with His seal. No matter how far afield a person wanders, he/she will someday acknowledge his/her connection with God. The Creator waits patiently for His beloved creations to return and even though backs are turned away from Him, The Divine Person still sends love and cares about us collectively and individually.

Be still and hear that guiding voice to direct you in wonderful ways and opportunities for growth. Originally He molded us in His image for He bequeathed us, each one, with royalty and all it entails. We, over the many lifetimes, lost sight of our divinity and struggled constantly instead of moving with the flow intended for us. We became wounded children not knowing where to turn and how to live. When we open up to our Creator, life begins for us as clearly as pure spring water, cleansing and renewing our spirit. True, trials still exist for this is a difficult place in which to evolve. And yet, we are evolving constantly, growing into a light-beam in God's plan for humanity. Accept this on faith for angels above see your light and rejoice that the earth controls you no more. When your soul reaches a point of spirituality, the mundane existence you once endured will serve you no longer. You know you are a child of God, and so you blossom wherever you are lighting up each place you enter. Be at peace knowing you are moving in the right direction and, when tribulation blankets the earth, you will know why and rejoice that mankind is returning to God. I am your comrade in the climb to perfection, Arcturus.

Pink flowers abound in God's kingdom. They represent every act of kindness and love given by every person on this wondrous planet, Earth. Pink is the color of love which radiates from the hearts of countless individuals who share their smiles, their time and their unselfish love with others. It is pleasing to Father/Mother God who allows more pink flowers in the garden of Heaven.

Be mindful of how you act and react to others keeping in mind that God sees your extension of His love to others who feel better because you acknowledged and cared. You are messengers of God's love and will ever share in passing on this love to all who come upon your path through life. Be still and allow an infilling of His love and then you can pass it on to those in need. Who knows that your action saves the life of one so dejected that they feel that to die is the only way out? Keep this in mind putting your transitory feelings of isolation or discontent aside so that you will allow many more beautiful pink flowers to pop up in your heavenly home to which you will one day retire. I am your friend and proponent of love always, White Buffalo Woman.

Fields of green flowing with the breeze are comforting to view. The expanse gives measure to your world for it promises largeness in your life. A field full of wildflowers in vibrant color allows the viewer to expand to a rainbow - colored inner world of magic and brilliance. And so Nature, resplendent with varied colors and depth, feeds the soul and brings a sense of completion to life.

Your job on earth is to emit your multi-colored and faceted inner being to those around you that allows a mingling of talents, gifts and inner beauty. At times you can bring solace to one who is at a low point in their life, and the same will be returned to you by another when you are down. And so it goes, the circle of life and its pleasant rewards given by a fellow human.

Animals play a large part in bringing happiness and joy to people who give love and attention to these wondrous gifts from God. How can one be lonely when a pet needs attention and love, and then it is reciprocated. The duty of a pet is to give affection in all forms to its owner, and that may be just their sweet presence by your side. They rely on you, and it makes you feel needed and loved. Open to this gift and be fulfilled as well.

Life is a meaningful journey from beginning to end. It is an adventure of vast proportions and gives impetus for growth in many, many ways.

And so I have shared my thoughts with you this beautiful, sunny, exceptional day. It is a pleasure to commune with you. I send blessings from our Master and from the Ascended Masters from whom you learn. I am your friend and proponent, White Buffalo Woman.

Caves are holes in the Earth, which open to the depths of Earth, and allow a home for many animals and creatures. They encircle them and make them feel secure from the dangers of life. They also provide an entrance to the riches of the Earth, such as gold, silver, and so many other blessings to mankind.

The depths of your being hold treasures and blessing to others, as well. When you open your heart to the God Presence to fill it with His being, you are containing treasures beyond any you will find in the Earth, for when the light fills your soul, it will heal every particle of darkness, hurt, or injury that remains there to block your exchange with others. While you allow this light of the I am to permeate your being by calling for the Violet Flame to fill you, you are dissipating the negativity that still holds you in areas of your being. Open wide the doors of your heart that the I am can fill you and give you joy and happiness that will inundate you that all might see the light radiating from you to all about you.

When this happens, you are able to give forth the sweet essence of pure love that comes from the I am Presence and touches others in a special way. It is not you, Dear Ones, but the God within that allows others to respond to you. Spread His light, and you will find true peace, joy, and happiness filling every day of your life. I am White Buffalo Woman and hold you all dear to my heart.

Dewdrops cover the ground in the early morning, giving nourishment to plants and flowers as well as little creatures that scurry to and fro, seeking food and water. God, the Almighty One of the Universe, provides for His creations in special ways, for his plan is so simple and yet complex. Trust in Him for your daily needs and, yea, your wants as well. Be as a little creature or a little child in your attitude of trust and faith, and you will receive abundantly until your hands and your heart is full to overflowing with His love and gifts. How fortunate you are to know of His great love, for so many do not and wander in the wilderness disconsolate and dejected not by their Creator, but by their own selves.

Sparkle brightly in His radiant light, allowing His light to shine through you to others. Think of the crystals that have become so popular. They are multifaceted, and they transmit light like a prism with myriad colors and textures. God will shine through you this way using your special gifts and talents. You are meant to reflect His light, helping one another in your daily journeys. Be like the crystal––pure and clear, filled with God's special reflection shining forth for the edification of others about you.

Think of the radiant sun shining into all the dark, dank corners, dispelling darkness and cleansing the air, purifying it as it filters through the dust particles lingering there. You can reflect the light of the I am and act as a purifier. Joined together, you, as light bearers, can penetrate the density and darkness around you, dispelling it in the same way. Be open, Dear Ones, to the light of God. Be receptive to the grace that pours continually to all creation from a loving Creator. You have no idea, Dear Children, how much your Father-God loves you. See how a loving father gently touches the face of his child, and you will begin to understand your Father-God's love. I am your teacher and friend, St. Germain, welcoming you into the light of the I am.

The third eye is opened more fully as you open to the Masters, angels, and, of course, your Mighty I am Presence. It is the key to knowledge that directs you to eternity, for when you open your mind and heart to training from on high, you automatically stimulate your third eye and pineal gland, from whence divine inspiration and life itself flows through you, around you, and out to others. You become a divining rod that is like a bright light penetrating the darkness around you. Increasing awareness, you are then able to follow the leadings and pursue all that will lead you on to your quest for oneness with the I am. Furthermore you will be more able to assist others who walk about with scales over their eyes. They are unable to see the purpose of their existence, for it is not to live meaningless, empty lives, clamoring after more wealth, sex, or worldly pleasures that will never satisfy the longing in their heart for oneness with their Creator-God. This longing, Dear Ones, is a gift, for it instills in one the prod to joy, peace, and true meaning of life, which is to return to your place within the great heart of Father/Mother-God. Filling the void, the Ascended One once again holds the answers to all questions. All the veils are drawn aside, and the soul is in tune with the heartbeat of his/her Creator. Be vigilant, Dear Ones, that you do not stray from the path, for it is tempting to follow other leadings, which will pull you away from the main road to freedom and glory. I am your friend and guardian, St. Germain. Allow us to fill your minds, hearts, and bodies with healing from our dear I am Presence.

New eggs, before they hatch, lay dormant and seemingly lifeless, but when the chick inside is ready to break forth from his warm abode, he pecks at the wall and steps out into the sunlight. So it is with you, Dear Ones; you are in preparation for the outer world, and the warmth and security you feel will prepare you for the world outside. You will peck away, so to speak, at the walls that separate you from others, and soon the barriers will be removed, and you will communicate with others more easily. Patience is paramount to this preparation period, for when you break out too soon, you will not be able to cope with the harshness of the elements and will perish, for your strength will not be sufficient.

Abide in the protection of others who are like-minded, and the warmth you feel is God's love shared by all. Others in the outer world are not aware and receptive to God's presence, and so they are cold and lost so far away from God's love. It will be your job to show them God's warmth and love dwelling within you, and then they will awaken and accept the Gift of the I am within them that lights the flame of love for each of them. I am Arcturus, the messenger of God's grace sent to you. Rest in His love this day.

Life is a fleeting moment in time, but it can be used to great advantage when one reaches a place of acceptance of the God Presence, for that gives meaning to every act accomplished in living. You feel the light around you and in you, for you are literally moving in God. Keep your mind in a positive mode, for it brings in light to help you in your daily life. It makes no sense to mouth prayers and not have desire to change in your heart. Continue to look to God within those around you, for it makes life so much more pleasant; does it not? It is time for you to relate to each person you encounter through the God in you and in them. All extraneous feelings melt when the light comes into your presence. Others feel this and immediately go into high gear (as a car) in order to move up to a level wherein the light shines brighter.

I have told you this world is dense. (You can see it with your inner eye.) But it ascends to a greater level of clarity when God's presence is honored. That is why you feel good in homes of some and in the presence of many people. You must choose your close friends with care and discernment, for the only way you will find happiness and even joy is in the presence of Godly people. True, you must be among people to spread God's light and word but that does not mean you spend leisure time and resting time with those whose intentions are not focused on the light of God, for then you begin to pick up their feelings and ways and descend deeper into the denseness of this world. Instead it is far greater to live and associate with those of like mind and concentrate on the Almighty I am Presence.

Go in peace this day with God's light around and in you. We are even now protecting you. St. Germain.

"I am" is the mightiest statement in the universe, for it created the universe and all in it, including you all, my Dear Children. I am Arcturus and wish to speak with you today.

In the great cosmic plan you hold a place dear to God's heart, for you, each one, will contribute to the victory for many. Your minds concentrate and focus on this path in an unusual way. You see, not all are able to do this. Your lights will shine brightly because of this concentration on the Mighty I am Presence. We Ascended Masters are here to assist you, for we see the light in and around you, which gets brighter every day. As you open more to our direction, you will be able to be used more for one follows the other. The need is great and the workers are few, Dear Ones. We do so much to assist mankind, but it is evident that those who are willing to be used to help others are of great use to us, for you can reach some who could not be reached any other way. When you see negativity and darkness in individuals, do not walk away. Instead allow the light of God, the Magic Presence, to flow to them, for have we not told you recently that light chases away the darkness? Ah, so!

Hold fast to the promises the I am has made to you, and you will truly be filled with joy, peace, happiness, and most of all, love!

You needn't descend, Dear Ones, to anyone's level if they are courting darkness. You have but to focus on the I am and the light of protection, and perfection will cover you. Stay in your own power of the I am, and you will float in serenity and peace, though chaos and darkness are a step away. Isn't this a marvel to you? It should certainly give you much to think on, Dear Ones. And so I take my leave and place my blessing upon you. Someday we will meet face-to-face, and the joy we have will be in the divine.

Have joy and peace around you this day no matter what comes by you.

All the green leaves on every tree in the world do not add up to "infinity." I, your Father/Mother God, have created all there is from my Self for I have been forever and will be forever. I know it is hard to place this concept in a world of time in which you exist, but it is true and you, being a part of me, also enjoy infinity and eternity for there is no such thing as "time" here. We live just beyond the veil that separates the two "worlds" of existence. This is another mystery to you. Since so many live in their minds, it is easy to dismiss that which you cannot see. Those of you who live in your hearts and accept with blind faith that I exist and the place you call heaven does as well, will be most at peace.

When you pass from the life you are enjoying, you will "see" what I say is true. There are so many, many truths that you find hard to comprehend, but someday soon you will see I am speaking of an existence you will truly love.

Most babies at birth cry loudly their protest of living again for they sense they will miss this blessed home called heaven. But remember this, for it is indeed truth, you chose to reincarnate for your soul's growth because there is nowhere that you can grow as quickly as you can on Earth.

When you are born you immediately feel the weight of the atmosphere knowing you've returned again to live on this very dense planet. Dense is the best word to describe earth for it is true. The earth is very dense because of the lingering results of centuries of abusive acts inflicted by humans living on earth. The beauty of this planet is palpable to each who soak in its life. But always there is the feeling that pleasure is fleeting, and one will be bombarded with the opposite very soon.

When you are in rapture over its beauty, such as The Grand Canyon or Yosemite, draw that moment in to your memory for it will help you during hard, dark times and experiences.

Do not take in negativity that permeates television, movies and the like. Instead be very selective in what you view and hear for these senses are very powerful and lingering thoughts and sights dwell within for a long time. It is good that they diminish with time, but why take them at all?

Love allows you happiness so stick to giving and receiving love. Louis Armstrong's popular song, "What a Wonderful World" was divinely inspired for it sums up so much of what I am trying to say. Hear it and see what I am saying for it typifies what love is all about – love of the earth and one another.

Open your hearts, minds and the gifts of hearing and sight and go into this day with love foremost in your thoughts. I will give you love to share with others. Just ask and receive for I love you very, very much.

I am your Father/Mother God coming to you this lovely day.

Do you not weep when you see inequities? Do you feel sad when you hear of injustices inflicted upon men, women and children? Does your heart ache for those whose lives are being taken in distant lands for merely standing up to their oppressors? Then harken to my words for I wish to speak for these few who suffer grave injustice.

When one person is oppressed, all are oppressed for all are connected as I have said before. You think you are alone? No, you are not. If you feel you can continue your way of life even though children are starving and being used for vile pleasures (and it's happening right under your nose and not only on the other side of the world) then your thinking is far afield from where it should be. Does it not warm your heart to see people being honored and cared for by groups who have heart? It is really what all should do, reach out and touch the lives of those in need. You cannot turn your head aside any longer for now is the time to start helping others in their plight and suffering. If one is hungry, you must share what you have. If another is sick, you must tend to their needs in whatever way you can. Does it hurt to smile and lend a hand? No, it does not. What hurts is you turning away from those in need. How cruel it is to turn aside and fill yourself with food and the comforts of life you enjoy but overlook the struggles of many about you. Share, dear ones, and see how content and happy you will feel.

I admonish you to act with kindness, love and compassion for those in need about you. You do not have to go to a faraway land, but open your eyes and see those who are in want about you. It could be that one only needs attention or it could require some sacrifice of time, food or money for the least desirable nearby. What does it take to move about in love not judging everyone you meet? I allow all their station in life that their soul will grow through their individual experiences. Their soul growth is the goal for each life chips away at the veneer exposing the pure soul created by me. Eventually all will blossom into a perfect pure, white flower befitting your God-nature. You will return to me as a clear vessel of love which is how I intended you to be from your very first step of life.

Now, my dear children, open your hearts to a higher purpose and reach out to your fellow humans with love and kindness and good thoughts to help them if they stumble so that it can come back to you when you falter or fall. I love all my creations and desire only good and happiness for each one. Open your hearts and allow love in so it can be given to all you meet each day. My love is always there for you. Return to my side for an infilling of this love that you can share it with all. Blessings to you this day.

CHAPTER FIVE

SEE ME IN OTHERS

Checkers is a game you play for fun, and in this game the object is to take as many pieces as possible from your opponent. It is a competitive game that teaches one to win and defeat another. Many games children play teach competitive behavior, and early you are taught that competition is the way of life as you know it. It is a very difficult task to unlearn this competitiveness and learn sharing and combining talents for the betterment of all. You see even as children you have learned that competition is the way of life, when indeed it is farthest from the truth to a happy, productive nourishing existence, in which all are happy and working toward a common goal. Even your educational system reinforces that which you learn from your parents, siblings, and companions. It is a difficult thing to unlearn that which has been ingrained in you, but it is necessary to do so in order to be deeply happy and content. You are responsible for those with whom you interact each day. You must love them and desire to serve them in whatever way the interchange demands. Even a smile may be all that is necessary, but it sends love to them, and they walk away a little more at peace because you showed them kindness. Harmony, Dear Children of the Light, begins with you. When you show love in small acts of kindness, then you are spreading harmony, and it moves forward in concentric circles that flow out to many others. Live in peace and share God's love that fills your heart. An infilling of love from the I am is always there, ready to inundate you and fortify you to act justly, lovingly, and positively to all you encounter each day. Be comforted knowing that you need only "be" to allow God's love to flow through you to others. This releases the competitive instincts ingrained in you and others. Go in peace and allow God's love to flow through you to others.

When clouds cover your Earth, it seems the sun is not there any longer, but you know this is not true, for you accept on faith that it is still shining above you. So it is with life. Sometimes it feels as though the sun is no longer there, that the Father/Mother-God has left, but it is not so. Accept on faith that your I am is always with you and in you, for it is true. He directs your life as you allow Him that privilege. Always be mindful of God's presence in your life so that solutions will come faster than problems.

Now we ask you to take this concept one step further. God is in you, but He is in every person, place, and thing in creation. Love the God that dwells in all, and you will be empowered to love each person, animal, and inanimate object you deal with each day. Tell them you love them, not necessarily vocally, but by your actions toward all. There is a saying you use on Earth, and it is so true——"Actions speak louder than words." Act out of love and in love in all you do, and say, and even think, and you will be happy, prosperous, and fulfilled in this life and beyond. Strive for perfection, for it is indeed within your grasp, for God, the Almighty One of Heaven, dwells in your midst.

When you view a beautiful sunrise or sunset, a beautiful flower or animal, a wondrous work of art, or listen to pleasing music, the feelings you have are a form of worship. Spend your days appreciating your surroundings and seeing the beauty all around you, and happiness will stay with you always. Open your eyes, ears, and heart ever wider to accept God's creations ever deeper in your soul and mind, and you will find peace around you always. Step into this day expecting and anticipating that life will be sweet, and, Dear Ones, it will be. I am St. Germain, your teacher and friend, encouraging you to live more fully this day and always.

Mountains and hills in the distance appear blue, purple, or grey, but when you come closer to them, you see they are browns, greens, and earth tones. The atmosphere of course causes your eyes to see something that is not so. It is an illusion. Extend this to many other things in life, for much is illusion. It isn't what it appears to be.

The gift of discernment is to help you choose the correct path. It will help you choose people who will be good friends with whom you can grow and change into more perfect beings. Life has its lessons, and there are times when they will be hard lessons. That is often when you grow faster, for you must look inside for answers since your mind has not been able to "see" what is best for you. There is nothing that will overcome you unless you allow it. Each lesson will pass, and a new one will be on the horizon. It too will be clouded until you come closer to the problem or happening. Then look inside for answers and most of all discernment. Your guardian angel will help you in your decisions if you will open up to this magnificent gift of God.

If you could see the light around you that comes from your Mighty I am Presence, you would be in awe, Dear Ones. We, the Ascended Masters, see the beautiful light around you and rejoice, for as you open more to your Godhead, you are filled with a wondrous light that is the God-Substance within you. A newborn baby is awesome to behold, for it has the glow of God-Light emanating from its being. It has just left the other world where the light of the I am is so vivid, and he/she retains much of it still. Even if the child is ugly by world standards, it is still beautiful to behold, for we sense the light filling its little body. Some children hold this light for many years, and the beauty of God shines through. Artists often paint children, for they are indeed a fascination. This is what Christ meant when He said you must become as a little child filled with the light of the I am, innocent and trusting of the Father-God. You can allow the light to shine brighter through the decrees and meditative states. I am St. Germain asking you to open to the light more each day.

CHAPTER SIX

GOLDEN LIGHT OF THE I AM

(At Beaver Creek – Sedona, Arizona)

The trickling sound of this little creek is a reminder that God's love flows constantly to you, for as this stream must flow so does His flow to you in a constant stream. You are blessed, Children, for you are opening up to receive the mighty flow of love, and it will change you forever. You must understand that His desire is for all to open to His love, flowing steadily down upon His created ones. It will be your job to show others this mighty stream of love 100 × 100 more powerful than this tiny stream. Can you imagine this? A flowing ocean of love descends and fills the hearts of those who are open to His love. Visualize this mighty ocean of love flowing upon you, and you will be bathed completely in this wonderful love.

I am St. Germain, your guardian, teacher, and friend. The time is coming when you will rely on the steady stream of love to sustain you and keep you in His care and protection, for times will be difficult, and you will need to be surrounded and upheld by His love. The people of Earth have turned their backs on the Almighty and have caused a turbulent existence in which they feel lost and in despair. You were there not so long ago. Now you have returned and are much more at peace in your heart. It will increase to a point that you will be instantly aware of the I am in your being. This will allow you to move through life easily.

You see this stream before you. Notice how it just flows, despite obstacles which slow it down in spots, and yet it finds an exit and continues to flow. Small sections are waylaid and are stagnant, but eventually even those parts will flow, for the gentle rains will come and increase the flow, bringing the stagnant area along. The gentle rain from heaven is the grace of God you hear about. It is actually the compassion of the Almighty flowing down upon those in need. If you were to see little ones suffering, would you not in your humanness have compassion? Then, Dear Ones, how much more our Creator, Father-God, has for each of His created children when they are stagnant in their lives or suffering in their hearts, souls, and bodies. Miracles are but an outward manifestation of the compassion and love of the Almighty One.

As God's great love fills your being, soul, heart, and body, you too will be able to work miracles for your fellow travelers for God's love will go out to those in need, and they will find what they are seeking. You are soldiers in training, for you will be entering a battle against evil with which mankind shrouds itself. Pure love dispels evil and darkness, for light and love will not allow them to remain for light and love scatters them away.

Continue to raise your face to the love of God, and He will bless you with His light, which will fill you to overflowing. The golden light descending from your Godhead into your heart and body will renew you daily, for it remains at work within. Keep your thoughts elevated, and you will be flooded with golden light and the love of God every minute of every day. Be at peace this day. Our love and care surround you.

Heather dots the hills in Scotland, just as cactus does in Arizona. Each part of the planet has flowers and vegetation that is found primarily in that region. It feels comfortable to see these plants growing around you when you live in a certain place on Earth. The familiar is comfortable always to individuals, whereas the unfamiliar is strange and sometimes forbidding. And so it goes with all beings on this planet. Individuality is the call word and mode of life for nearly all the inhabitants of Mother Earth. It makes life very difficult because there is a lack of unity, and you feel as though you are on your own. That is why relationships are so important here on this planet. People spend their entire lives searching for the perfect relationship. The perfect relationship does not rest in an individual, but in the God Presence which dwells within. Once that relationship is established, then it is possible to form lasting connections with others of like mind. It is essential to do so, Dear Ones, in order to find peace and serenity. Then it matters not where on Earth you are placed, for you carry this knowledge of the Divine Presence, the I am, within your heart, mind, and soul, and you have reached enlightenment. All things fall into place when one attains this level of consciousness, and externals do not matter as they once did.

You see how humans involved in earthquakes react to things now that they have experienced such total destruction around them. They are happy to have life and another opportunity to move on in lessons and life's challenges. I say to you that they will no longer be the same, for they have brushed with death and have been spared. This will be repeated in many parts of the world, and the consciousness of mankind will be changed forever. This is only the start, Dear Ones, for life is fragile, and the life of Mother Earth is way out of balance due to the lack of respect and greed of so many. This year is a pivotal year for Earth's inhabitants. Changes will be rapid and complete, and no longer will passivity and ambivalence work. Individuality will not work either, and groups must join together for survival. Creation awaits this cleansing, for out of the rubble will rise a new consciousness in all who survive. A new age will dawn that has never been known on this planet. I am Arcturus, and I encourage you to pray for all mankind.

When you were very young, you took a buttercup and held it under your chin to see if you love butter. The reflection of the yellow indicated that you did. Now apply this to your life. The reflection of God, the Mighty I am, within you is shining out for others to see and know you are indeed a child of God.

Feelings of unworthiness must be laid aside, for remember this: Each person is a child of God and worthy to be filled with God's light. Be willing to show others the path back to the I am. The warmth you feel inside is the God Presence. Now share the love and light with others. Bring the wondrous news that God does indeed live, for He dwells within all. Though he cannot be seen by the naked eye, He dwells in all nonetheless. The beauty of flowers, majestic mountains, and little puppies so full of exuberance reflect His light and love. The kindnesses shown to you by others are a reflection of His love. All creative, beautiful sights and acts are reflections of God's light and love. Begin to recognize the I am in all you see, the music you hear (even the music of nature, such as birds chirping or coyotes howling), and the touch of another who shows God's love to you in little, subtle ways. Live this way also that God's light and love will abound in your lives. I am White Buffalo Woman greeting you this day.

If you were to stand tall up on the highest mountaintop and turn 360 degrees all around, what would you view? The entire world is filled with the Creator essence and contains the I am whom you recognize and honor within yourselves. God is in all and allows all to run smoothly over the course of life. The life of God is within all, Dear Ones, and this bears repeating. You cannot look one way or the other without viewing the I am. Remember this, Dear Children, and you will see Him in each person you meet. This is a lesson that bears repeating for humans. Being human of course, we tend to forget this fact. When you do remember that the I am dwells within each person, you can relate easier and better to another. Hold that thought in your minds this day, and see if it doesn't help you relate better to those you meet. I am Arcturus, your ally and teacher.

I am White Buffalo Woman in your presence today, for I have a message for you and your friends. We see your hearts and know you are sincere in your efforts to honor the Almighty I am Presence. This is good. Now we will show you a more perfect way to come into His presence more fully. See the I am in your hearts, for the golden light coming from your Godhead fills you with healing and love that is the Mighty I am. Now that you are bringing this light from above you into your beings through your heart, the seat of your soul, you are bringing the I am into a closer, real, tangible way that you might call forth His power and presence into your existence. In doing so, be mindful constantly of the golden light, the light of the I am, in your very being. This should be very exciting to you, for now your I am is as near to you as your heartbeat, and it is just as important to your lives, especially your spiritual lives, my Dear Ones.

Let His presence become so real to you that with every heartbeat, you will feel His being within yours, and you will call Him forth into all your human activities, large and small. You can be victorious in this life right now because of the closeness of the Almighty I am. Be mindful, Dear Ones, that you are children of the light, and as such you can walk through all sorts of danger and darkness and not be affected or harmed. The Almighty I am will become so real to you that you will converse with Him and know things about life that otherwise would slip by you. He will show you constantly what you must do and say, for you have given Him your lives, and He wishes to work through you, bringing light, love, and care from the Almighty I am. Blessings to you, Dear Ones.

I am White Buffalo Woman come to you this day.

Green fields glowing with the radiant light of the I am are meant to be part of your life in which to roam and play. The little daisies and other jaunty, little flowers bob before you as you wander the path of delight. Relax, Dear Ones, and enjoy God's wondrous gifts of beauty that beckon you to play and romp in the luxurious gifts of nature. Open your eyes and your minds to accept all the gifts that come to you from the I am. It is through nature's treasures that you begin to see and feel that you, too, are a treasure in the coffers of the King, the I am, your Father-God. Look within, Dear Children of the Light, for therein lies something more magnificent than any worldly riches, for you contain the spark of life––the glorious golden light of the I am. If this is so, and it is of course, then,

Dear Ones, don't you see what a gift you are to one another? Keep in your minds and hearts this thought: You are a rainbow light to others, and they are the same to you. No man or woman is better or lesser than the other, for all are created likenesses of the Creator. Treat all with respect and love, and expect the same from others. I encourage you to walk with your head held high and your shoulders thrown back, confident and free in the knowledge that you are blessed and loved by the I am. Life can be glorious when you realize all creation is a gift. Enjoy the beauty that flows around you. Observe the rainbow and realize that same beautiful light is in your very core. You were not meant to be disconsolate, but to walk in confidence, and assurance, and most of all, peace. Love yourselves, Dear Ones, and then you can love life and all who pass your way.

I greet you with white roses in my hands, held out to you, each one.

The rose is a symbol of the soul, for it unfolds gently, emitting its sweet smell to all around it. And so, Dear Ones, is your soul unfolding as a beautiful rose as multicolored as you are, each one. Some are white for purity of intent and purpose. Others are red for the intense passion of your being as you do God's work. Some are a soft, gentle yellow for the calmness and gentleness of your soul. Others are a beautiful pink for the joy you give to others and for the beauty in your being. We see your souls unfolding and sending forth the sweet fragrance in a constant peaceful way to attract others to the God Presence within, just as a fragrant flower attracts honeybees and insects to it that pollination may occur, and many, many more fragrant, beautiful flowers may give glory unto their Creator. And so you are a garden of beautiful flowers for the King, our Creator-God.

Go about your daily tasks with full knowledge of who you are, Dear Children of the Almighty I am. Your chores will be light and happy, for you are bringing glory unto creation by your presence and the love that dwells within your heart. Life goes so smoothly when you claim your inheritance as children of the I am. The light surrounds you, healing all that needs to be healed in your body, mind, and soul. Continue your sacred tasks of love, and send the light out to others. Love one another, for a heart filled with divine love can do no different. I am White Buffalo Woman showering blessings upon you this day.

Summertime will be upon you soon. It will be much warmer, and you will bask in the sunshine, happy to be free of rain. The freedom from heavier clothing, which is an encumbrance, will allow you a lightness that you will feel more than you ever did in your past. The lightness comes from your prayers and meditations, too, for you are closer to your true self than ever before. The airwaves about you will seem to uphold you as if you were floating through life. This is really true, Dear Ones, for staying in the light allows you greater mobility, which helps you move easier through your daily duties.

Sewing good seeds produces an abundant crop, and the past year you have, each one, been planting a garden that will grow with time and flow out to others who will be fed from the overflow of God's love. You have no idea how far-reaching your care will go, for it creates a whirlwind of light that moves with you even after your joint prayer time. You are all surrounded with a white light that is the explosion of the I am within you, for you have concentrated on decrees for others, and it has greatly increased your own aura, which portrays your inner light.

Accept this role as light bearers, for it is sorely needed in this world, particularly now. I have said often that weather patterns have changed, and you will see astounding displays of Mother Nature's renewal. The more light beings in an area, the greater the protection, for it is a way of cleansing that assists Mother Nature in her efforts at renewal. Often you will see violent storms centered about larger cities, for therein is much darkness and like always attracts like. Continue to pray for the Earth and its inhabitants that the grace of God will pour down upon the Earth in abundance. Then can many open to this wondrous light stream and be filled with God's light. This can change the force of storms, earthquakes, volcanoes, and such. I am St. Germain here to remind you to step up your prayers for the Earth.

CHAPTER SEVEN

LOVE, TRUTH, AND FAITH

You desire to know My Will? It is found in the recesses of your heart. Your mind holds My Thoughts. You have only to trust that I am leading you step-by-step as I have instructed you to walk. Slowly I will lead you so that you will not stumble and fall because you move too quickly, too haltingly. Hold My Hand and I will lead.

Love is the healing balm My Children need––love for me. Reach out for me in love, My Love that abounds in your heart. Love heals. Love soothes, calms, and restores. Ask for My Love, and I will give you an abundance, overflowing––going out to others and renewing those open to My Loving Touch.

Truth is from me because it brings all into My Light. My Light shines brightly where truth is spoken and held in esteem. Truth frees, unlocks doors, and penetrates dark corners.

Faith comes through trusting. Clinging to me and only me will keep faith whole and alive.

Joined together, *love, truth,* and *faith* in me will win victory after victory. Evil cannot withstand this combination, for it tears down and destroys walls. Evil cannot prevail against My Spirit of Love, Truth and Faith dispersed through My Chosen Ones. Stand firm. Love, speak truth, and have faith in me and My Promises.

Go forth in My Armor, My Protection. I will shield you and guide you. Love me, My Child. Speak for me words of truth. Have full faith and assurance that I am, by rights, leading. Have you not asked me to lead? Trust then, implicitly.

Continue to learn My Way of Love so that you can teach others. To love with My Love is not impossible, but to love with a purely human love is like trying to give water with a sieve full of holes to men dying of thirst. It can never satisfy nor quench the thirst of anyone. To love with My Love should be your only concern. Reread I Corinthians 13, and you will know that human love can never do this. Take My Love into your hearts and forever be fulfilled.

Fireflies, dragonflies, butterflies, mosquitoes, and gnats flit and fly, light, and ascend, moving quickly, fluttering by, winding and wending their ways through the air. They soar and glide, doing as they were created to do, fulfilling God's plan for their existence.

You, Dear Ones, move through life in like fashion. You flit about, winding your way through the labyrinth called *life*. At times you descend or fly off on tangents, but at other times you fly and glide, soaring to wondrous heights, able to access the beauty about you, assessing your life in a moment before you light to walk through another phase, another lesson, another part of the blueprints you have chosen to plot your incarnation.

How wondrous is life with its many facets! Enjoy the beauty about you. Enjoy the companions and friends you have chosen. See the light in their eyes, the spark that is their God Presence. In fact make it a habit to see the Creator in all beings and creatures, for in doing so, you will be able to reach across and touch the I am. It is not an impossible task to honor all life and spread God's love. In doing so, you mingle with angels and saints. Let God's love fill your heart, your very being, and happiness will flood your soul. To fly through this life, love will be the air that sustains you, allowing you to soar to heights never before attainable. To love with human love is wonderful. To love with divine love is the epitome of existence, for in this pattern, you bring healing to those around you who sorely need solace, compassion, and the touch from the I am.

Step aside and let love flow through you to all you meet each day. It is as simple as flying is to a bird or butterfly. We call you to soar through life, not merely meander. You are called to live in harmony, and you will be happier and healthier as a result. Hallelujah. Praise be to the I am, the Almighty One of Heaven. I am Kathumi, master and servant, friend and guardian to those who seek for truth.

Praise me, for I alone am worthy of your praise. Put me first in your life above anyone or anything––jobs, money, pleasures. I desire to be first in your life now and forever. The days I give you on this Earth are limited, but limitless is the life you will lead in the hereafter. Humans cannot comprehend infinity, for it remains a secret to you. Think of the tiny grains of sand at the seashore, and still they don't reach an infinite number because infinity cannot be confined to a number.

Happiness in the afterlife is comprised of worshiping and loving me, your Creator. Happiness on Earth begins in the same, worshiping and loving me––but it goes beyond that to include those I give you to love and from whom you receive love. A heart filled with My Love is by its very nature ready and willing to love all it encounters, because I am in their midst. How happy the man who loves, because in the giving of love, an abundance is received, fulfilling my purpose in creating––unity in Love. I am the Alpha and the Omega––the beginning and the end––another mystery to mankind. Because I am, *you are,* because you and every creature are extensions of Myself.

Love those I send you to love. I will give you abundantly of My Love with which to encompass and encircle them. Do *all* in love, love for me. I will honor your attempts and increase your love 100 times 100. I have called you to love with My Love. Love for me.

The scent of a rose is the purest fragrance on Earth. It permeates your being with its delicate balance of pure light that mingles with the lasting memory of its essence. This delightful smell is a reminder of the I am from whence it flows, for it is a perfect example of the pure love God has for you. Breathe deeply of this gift, a reminder of the glories of creation.

Look about you in this beautiful place called Sedona, and absorb the vast wonder of the magnificent red rocks that glow with the kaleidoscopic transformation of the reflected light from the sun. Most powerful is twilight or sunset, for the hills radiate warmth, depicting the love of God that surrounds you, if you'll allow it.

Observe, Dear Ones, constantly, for you will always find new colors and pleasing sights that will thrill your being and soothe your soul. Once you discover the I am in such a personal manner, all life teams with a pulsating glow of eternity. You will never fathom totally how far-reaching is the stream of love from the I am, for it encompasses every facet of nature and every person that reaches momentarily into your space and time. Each incident is fleeting except for the few close loved ones you choose to interact with more totally. Grasp every opportunity to view another angle of the Creator-God, the I am, through the many personalities you deal with each day. You would not see that part of God except that you recognize another's beauty for a brief moment in time. The wonderful path of life is to be revered and enjoyed for its precious gifts to you. The wholeness of the I am comes to you more powerfully when you seize the moment and view the Face of God through the gifts given by others who know and love the I am, too. The spark of light you see in others is in the I am. Recall this when you deal with people this day. I am Arcturus, your friend and helper.

Wolves run in packs and are very loyal to one another. If one is in danger, the others rush to his aid and fight off all adversaries. This loyalty is to the death, if that is necessary. Wolves also mate for life and are faithful to their partners, helping to raise their babies and protecting their families at all costs. Humans could certainly learn much from these magnificent creatures of the wild.

Loyalty to one another is not always a human trait, for jealousy and envy are too strong in many a heart. Rise above this, Dear Ones, and give your loyalty and faithfulness to others of like mind. Stand by those you love and help them ascend on their journey to the light. The loyalty extends to the family of man, as well, for it is your calling to love all who come your way, not just those who have an attraction for you. Jesus called each to love all by treating them with respect. He asked that you rid yourself of resentments, bitterness, hatred, or any destructive feelings that remain in your heart and then go forth and give love, respect, and caring to all you meet. Yes, it is true you will have close friends and family for whom you will have a special caring and love, but what good is it if you cannot love all? It is easy to love those who return your love. It is not easy to extend your love to the entire family of man. This, Dear Ones, is what you are called to do––love all. How can you do this? Recognize the God Presence in yourself first and ask for His love to fill your heart to overflowing, and then you are able to love all who come your way with the pure love of the I am. We are here to assist you in your journey. Call on us for help, and we will be there in an instant. I am St. Germain and stand by you always. Remain in the light, Dear Ones, for therein will you find your strength.

Cling to those around you, for I have given you many to love and from whom to receive love. Do not reach out to people who are incapable of loving freely at this point in time. Suddenly My Spirit will penetrate the innermost areas of their hearts, where treasures are hidden. These jewels are particles of My Great Love. It is these perfect jewels of love that cannot be given easily and readily by some. These jewels of My Love should not be hidden in a cache, but should be freely given, for in giving I can pour more love into a heart to give again, and again, and again in a steady flow––a stream of compassion and love. It is this love that people long for. It is My Love that people need to survive. Child, it is My Love that you are seeking. I stand before you now to give you My Love. Open your heart to me that I might fill it with love so great that you will burn with the warmth that flows into your being.

My love heals. My love fortifies. My love renews and restores. I can make you whole as you open to My Love. Allow me to repair the wounds in your heart, for they are deep and jagged scars. My love flowing into these wounds will gently replace the scar tissue that mars the heart, rendering it incapable of total love and compassion for others. I mean to restore your heart that it might accept––that you will accept––the treasure that is My Love to flow, and flow, and flow into a heart that is new. Then and only then can you allow My Love to flow freely through you to others. Then you will be a channel of My Love, peace, and compassion. I mean to make you whole. I mean to restore you that I might use you. Your sensitivity will be honed and sharpened to such a clarity and sharpness that you will weep over inequities, you will weep over injustice, and you will bring solace to the victims of hatred, prejudice, and injustice. So great will be the flow of love that you will sigh. Your being will be an instrument of peace in a world of turmoil ridden with sin, sickness, and anguish. How sorely this world needs My Love! Do this for me, Child. Allow me to restore you and use you. I will be gentle, and you will be deeply happy and at peace. You have so much love locked up inside. Now let me help you learn how to give My Love. I will continue to inundate you with My Love, and you will respond by loving for me. Go now, for My Peace will be with you this day––this glorious day.

The mother deer is nurturing to her offspring in gentle ways when they are very young. As they grow she is stricter and restricts their movements and exuberance, for she is trying to teach them about the dangers they must deal with in their world. She knows there are predators that would harm or kill them and wishes to protect them at all times. All mothers share this instinct to love, nurture, and protect their young from danger. Love of course is the motivator, and one is blessed to have been loved and nurtured by his/her mother, for it allows the child the strength to face life and all its challenges. When children are not nurtured, they will wither and die or, worse yet, will carry this hurtful rejection into every aspect of their lives, causing much harm to others and sadness to themselves, for they cannot adjust or be happy for the gnawing hole inside will not be filled by anyone or anything. Only God's love can compensate and fill the gigantic chasm in their hearts. Until this happens to people such as this, nothing can touch them, for they lack the element in their hearts that is called compassion by some and conscience by others. Feeling secure and loved as infants allows people to, in turn, love themselves, and they can then reach out to others in love. When this cycle is broken at some point, these people are not able to function normally. When people have been neglected by their mothers, they may become so warped that they commit crimes against others and even become murderers or perverts, as well. Serial killers are often neglected and physically abused as children, so their sense of conscience is nonexistent. Teaching women to be loving mothers is lacking in this society, for the family unit is weak and in jeopardy. The answer is to work one-on-one with others who are in need of God's love to heal at soul level. The I am knowledge is sorely needed by many, many people, and we ask you to be open to helping others understand their destiny as children of God. I am St. Germain come to ask you to help those we send your way.

CHAPTER EIGHT

THE WONDER WITHIN

"I am the resurrection and the life." This is a powerful declaration, and you should use it whenever you think of it, for it opens the floodgates of Heaven and pours forth the power of the Almighty into your life and circumstances.

The use of this declaration is powerful because it declares your own resurrection and life, which will come about. This declares a victory over death and destruction, which occurs in your ascension, and that is what you will bring about through the constant use of the decrees. These are powerful, too, you see, and you are bringing the power of the I am into your lives. When you become more aware of your presence, you will be more victorious in your daily lives.

Few on Earth have ever recognized their I am Presence, and this is sad, for all you need to move through this life gracefully is within you and all about you. The decrees are a constant reminder that the I am dwells within you and all around you.

Jesus tried so many times to tell people that they only had to look within for answers to their questions and power for their lives, but they would not listen. The scholars were the worst offenders, for in their scientific, scholarly approach to life, they could not grasp the meaning of what the Christ was telling them. Jesus said, "Unless you become as little children, you shall not enter the kingdom of God." What did that mean?

Of course it meant you must be trusting as a small child to open to the simplicity of the profound statement that God dwells within. Trusting your Father in Heaven is trusting the God Presence that dwells within. It is that simple.

I wish for you to concentrate on your I am Presence every moment of every day, and then you will be completely at peace and happy, for you do not have to rely on your finite mind and ways. You have infinity within you! Allow me to elaborate on this statement.

The Creator created all you see and each person you know who dwells on this Earth and beyond from His own substance. Think of it . . . the light of God dwells in all and is all. It is such a profound truth that humans tend to limit themselves and life around them. It is truth, however, and to grasp it, you must open your minds and hearts as a little child and trust that God is all and in all. I will leave you with this thought today, and when you think on it, it will bring you one step beyond that you might understand more deeply your purpose in this great plan from a great and loving God. I am St. Germain. We are with you even now, the Ascended Masters and I. Greetings to all.

Beloved Children of God, you are growing very fast, for you have focused your attention on the Almighty I am. You are beginning to learn the power of the Presence, and it will hold you fast to His promise of life to its fullest and life everlasting. I am Sumat Kumara come to you this day to elaborate on the declarations of St. Germain, my friend and companion. We are taking you under our care to show you truths that you might spread them to others around you. You have said yes to our calling, cajoling, and drawing you into our presence to learn and to expand greatly in the power of the Presence. This is such a simple way, Dear Children, that many miss it and go through life as if they were robots neither looking to the right nor left, and most importantly, never looking within. How sad to see. The world's pleasures can never be appreciated until one looks within, sees the God Presence, allows the light to expand them, and then sees the beautiful creations with the eyes of the Creator. Do you begin to understand what this means, Dear Ones? You are appreciating the world of beauty through the eyes of God, for you are centering on His Being within you, and it is transforming you, each one, into a channel of love the likes of which most never know.

I spur you on, Dear Children of God, to new heights in the Almighty I am.

Oranges have a thick peel, which must be removed in order to get to the meat of the orange, the part that brings nourishment for the one partaking of its sweetness. You, too, Dear Ones, have a thick peel that must be removed little by little in order to allow your inner presence to be shared with others. You will each be used to bring nourishment to others, for in your inner core lies the I am presence, which lights you from within. How you adorn your body is not nearly as important as how you feed your inner spirit. It is necessary to look within for answers to all your questions, for within each one is the inner guidance needed to live through each day. By being centered, you will come to understand each happening, each dilemma, each glorious moment you draw into your life. Look at life as a magnificent opportunity to move closer to perfection, which comes from being close to your Father-God. The Spirit will direct you and bring comfort to your personhood. You are the highest form of creation, for you contain part of the Creator deep in your soul. Meditation allows you the privilege of being in touch with that part of your being. If it seems beyond you to understand, do not worry, for trusting that you are being led through this maze called life will put you at ease that you might fully enjoy the experience. Expect miracles to abound in your life, for this will happen as long as you trust the inner urgings, which come from deep within. Follow these urgings, and you will find success in every aspect of your life. I am St. Germain.

A blackboard is blank until you write messages on it. It is intended to be used to communicate knowledge, concepts, or pictorial representations of math or other sciences. It was an ingenious invention in its day and was used for many generations. It is now outdated for the most part, for there are more advanced methods of conveying knowledge. Foremost of course is a computer, which not only teaches but helps man in many, many other ways, as well. Its memory is fantastic in proportion to any invention man has opened to thus far. When you consider how it has changed life, you can see it has catapulted man into the future so fast humanity is suffering from jetlag, in a sense. It is almost beyond the thinking of man to realize the vast implications of the computer age. Just as airplanes, trains, and superspeed jets have decreased the size of the world and allowed greater communication and interaction, so has the computer shrunk the world again to allow an even higher level of the same. It is no longer possible to be isolated in this society man has created and allowed. Individuality is reduced, and man has begun to feel like a number, a robot at times, and suffers because of these new developments. How does one rise above this modern dilemma? The answer lies within your heart and soul, for therein is comfort in the Presence, the I am. This knowledge will allow you the privilege of knowing who you are, and whence you came, and most of all, where you are headed. You are not just a number, nor are you dispensable, as some feel mankind is. You are a child of the Creator and as such much loved and sacred because you are a part of God, the Almighty One. Think on this and it will change your life. Being positive is very important, for you will draw to yourself all goodness in every form. Like attracts like, and so it follows you must attract positive when you remain positive. How blessed you are to have this privileged information. I am St. Germain encouraging you to see the wonders of life.

Flowers you see around you are representative of the varied colors in the Creator's I am Presence, for they reflect the multicolored splendor that exists within you. When you see fields of daisies, realize that our God Presence is the Creator of all beauty, and flowers are a special part of the beauty given to us to enjoy. When you hold a rose in your hand next time, really peruse it and examine the intricacy and delicacy of its beauty, and you will begin to see how wondrous is the God who created all the flowers and the beauty we see each day.

Oh, Dear Ones, open your eyes and notice the wonder of creation, and then you can begin to see the complex magnificence of your Creator, the same, very same, Mighty I am Presence within you. How incredible is this thought, Dear Ones.

I am Arcturus, and I wish to converse with you this day. I desire that you begin to appreciate the awesome nature of the I am, for, you see, God's Presence is such an overpowering delight, and He dwells within your very being. It is always a wonder to a human to realize that the Creator is in all––every person, every magnificent sunset, every leaf and flower, every raindrop that joins with others to sustain life. Consider the beauty of everything around you, and you will just turn the first page in the book of God's stupendous account of creation. How glorious is our Creator, Dear Ones. Begin to think on this today, and when you see something that moves you because of its variegated splendor, remember the same Creator dwells within your very being. You are children of the light and beings of joy to your Father–God, for you give Him the honor and praise He rightfully deserves. Continue this path you have chosen, for it will surround you with a rainbow of light at all times, and you will certainly find the pot of gold at the end of the trail, for your ascension is assured when you recognize and give honor to the Almighty I am. Recognition is the first step toward comprehension, and in comprehending the splendor of the Almighty, you must certainly give Him praise and honor.

When you were very small, colors were very vivid to you, and life was an adventure of great proportions. Romping and playing in the grass, fields, and forests, you were enthralled by the wonder of life. This freedom you felt was the joy of life overflowing into all activities. The butterflies, ants, and animals all about you held your undivided attention. Even the little mice in their nests captured you for quite a time, as did the rainbows in the sky, the flowers in the field, and the warmth of the sun as you lay in the grass and wondered at the figures in the clouds. Each morning was a new calling to wander freely, exploring the teeming life about you. As the years flowed past, you came to see things differently and in fact often did not "see" at all. Soon the cares and woes of responsibilities and complicated days began to wear heavily upon your mind. Relationships grew more intense and even devious at times. We ask you to return to your youthful exuberance and begin to see the beauty of nature all about you. Take time to romp and play in the sunshine and grow closer to the Earth and its treasures. Become as the little child you once were, and release your cares that in your trusting of the Presence, you will find more solutions than problems. People complicate their own lives. No one does it for you. Be simple in your demands of life and selves, and trust all good will come your way, and it will be so. You will be as magnets drawing to yourselves peace, joy, happiness, and much love. Centering on the I am that dwells within, you will be once again carefree and joyful, for you will see with renewed sight all the beauty you have overlooked for such a long time. By returning to the ways of your childhood, you will become childlike in your expectations of life. Trusting in your heavenly Father, you can release all tension and worry to Him. Live each day to the fullest, and this will give praise to the One who made you and who continues to dwell within you. I am White Buffalo Woman, a friend and guardian spirit.

Clarity of purpose is important to establish within yourself, for there is no room for duplicity. The Almighty I am Presence, once recognized and honored, changes the awareness of your being and life force, for you realize you are being led by a higher source that encompasses every fiber of your body and soul. If you will honor His presence and call Him into your daily life, miracles can then abound, and your very thinking will change. Some call it miraculous, but it is only divine law working within you.

The I am Presence is a fact, Dear One, and you only have to focus your attention upon Him, and you will live life to its fullest and have abundance, for you have but to ask and all good things will rise before you, honoring the Divine Presence and coming to your assistance. Life is beautiful once you concentrate on the I am, for a golden light begins to shine around you, for you cannot contain this light any longer when you center on its source, the Almighty I am Presence.

Dear Ones, I call you this day to service. If you answer my call (for it comes from God, you see, and not just from me), then you will be surrounded with angels and beings of light who will protect you, guide you, and direct you to the One who is to be honored and served. You cannot serve two masters, for if you serve God, the Mighty I am within you, then you cannot continue to serve the worldly powers that are only out to destroy your soul.

I call you to service this day, and if you answer yes, then I, St. Germain, will teach you daily how to live more fully in the divine, which *is* your birthright and privilege, for you are a child of God and heir to the kingdom of light, which you would see is magnificent if you could glimpse it. The joy in your soul will expand to include all life around you. All the petty, insignificant annoyances will vanish as if by magic, and it is magic in a sense, for it is the Magic Presence changing you little by little, and sometimes quickly, so much so that those you have not seen for a time will marvel at the changes you will display.

I call you to service. Are you ready and willing to clothe yourself in the white garments of the Almighty and step forth into a new life, one which will be so joy-filled that you will not be able to contain the happiness it gives, and you will have to give it to those you meet each day? That is the life I and the Almighty I am call you to. Will you answer yes? Ponder this in your heart and quietly answer the call.

Our love to you this day. The Ascended Masters and I rejoice at your progress and growth and are here this moment urging you forward into a new life of service to God. I am St. Germain.

CHAPTER NINE

HALLS OF FREEDOM

Acorns do not fall far from the tree. It was part of the mother tree for so long that it is exactly like it, and so it perpetuates the cycle and becomes a mighty oak tree, eventually. People are much the same, for genetically they are much like their parents and in their thinking, as well. That is why an incoming soul carefully selects his/her parents-to-be, for he/she will be in an environment to learn the lessons his/her soul must learn. It also follows that the child is very much like his/her parents emotionally and many, many other ways, as well.

The important factor that separates a child from his/her parents is free will, for that is a gift from God that allows the child to be a free agent able to make decisions that might be totally contrary to what his/her parents might accept or understand. There is always a generation gap, but what that really means is that the child is capable of making choices that affect his/her life, thrusting the child into the arena of life as a free being exercising the privilege of free will.

Life is a learning place, and often a person must experience all types of lessons in order to grow and become aware of his/her station in life, and the consequences of the choices will be good or bad. Even God will not interfere with free will, for He values this gift He has given His children and encourages each one to see its value, as well.

Now for how this affects you, Dear Ones. You have many roads before you. Some lead to great success, and others lead to turmoil, despair, and the like. Listen to the inner voice of your higher self, for it will guide you each step of the way if you will turn to this guidance. You will be encouraged strongly to choose ways that will advance you and bring you great joy and happiness. Your inner urgings will try to show you a more perfect way. Meditate, listen, and follow these messages, these urgings, and you will find great joy at the end of the way. I am Arcturus bringing you encouragement and blessings this day.

The red, white and blue of the American flag are symbolic of the great glory of this land. The red is for the blood shed by so many to make and keep America free. The white is for the purity and perfection of the original intent of the Constitution and cause of freedom. The blue is for loyalty to God and justice always. You see how far away from the original concepts of life America has wandered? It is our intent, the Ascended Masters and I, St. Germain, to bring this land back under the mantle of the I am and bring justice, love, freedom, and the desire to worship God back to America and the peoples of this land. It must rise as a shining light so bright to the other nations of the world that all will take up America's example once again and follow her to freedom and perfection. It is through this divine example and way that this world can be saved. Mankind is on the brink of glory or disaster. It could go either way, but your prayers and decrees are heard and can tip the balance in the direction of life and love. It is imperative that you pray daily for America's freedom and life, for she needs assistance to find God once again and be loyal to the concepts originally set down for this country. We work constantly to bring America out of the clutches of evil's darkness into the light of God's plan for this beautiful land of freedom and love.

We are with you in your endeavors to pray for and help to save this land for God. Hold fast to your dreams of a land filled with light that will continue forever on the path of freedom. Blessings to you, Children of the Light. We are with you this day. Call on us for assistance whenever you need help.

Lo, how mighty is the power of the I am to bring light, love, and freedom to the people of America. This is a blessed land, and that which is not of the light will be dissolved. Continue to pray for this land you presently call home. There will come many changes to this world and its people, and those of the light will be protected. Continue to pray with others and by yourself, as well, for these prayers and decrees will bring more light to this beloved land, and she will shine as a bright star, a diadem, a beacon light for all the world. Do you realize how much America is a light to the world even now? It is true, Dear Ones, and this will increase through your prayers and decrees. Light obliterates darkness, and the more light you bring within this land, the greater will America become as a force for good in a world gone mad.

Egotism and greed are at the root of the problem in this world. Those who are in control, and they are many, choose to stamp out freedom, free will, and choice and cause the people of the world to be slaves, robots to their selfish desires to rule all people of the Earth under one law, one rule, one domain.

The I am will not allow this, for even He will never overrule free will. The Earth changes will sweep away this possibility, and woe to the ones who are attempting this world order! They will bring destruction to themselves, for what you send out, Dear Children of the Light, comes back to you a hundredfold. Send out your light, your love of the I am, to everyone around you, and you will receive the same. I am St. Germain come to you to enlighten you a bit more this day.

The Good Shepherd leads His sheep and forever guides them and surrounds them with protection. The Good Shepherd is the I am Presence within you and has always protected you and tried to guide you into the Light. There were times when you preferred the darkness, and in that darkness you met wolves and predators that attempted to destroy you. Now you are walking in the light once again, and your protection from the I am is ever present around you. Stay in that light and you will see and feel the glory of God.

I am St. Germain, and I wish to speak with you this day. Halls of freedom are where you dwell as long as you recognize and honor the I am. You have no idea what this means as yet, but it will be revealed to you little by little. Remaining in the Presence and decree work will bring you ever closer to the brilliance of the I am in and around you. It is always there–– the Light of God––but you are not always aware of it. Concentration in and through prayer allows you to feel the warmth of the light and to see the light in everything and everyone around you. Victory is the gift of the I am, for He leads you as a Good Shepherd and consoles you when you are down and binds your wounds when you are injured in any way. His care for you is obvious when you but open your eyes and view your life situation. Expect good, and it will be drawn to you as if to a magnet. Rest well, Dear Ones, in the knowledge that you are loved and cared for by the I am. Blessings will abound in your life this day.

Today you will be free to choose your path as you are always free to do. Freedom of choice and will is a gift from the Almighty One within each of you. Chains will never bind you to go one way or the other. If God Himself does not bind you, then you are not to bind one another either. You must meet each one in freedom, and when one attempts to bind you, you must not allow it. I am St. Germain, your teacher and friend.

Today is a glorious day for it allows you another opportunity to spread God's light, love and His word of freedom. In order for you to tell these wondrous truths, you must feel them strongly yourselves. Absorbing this knowledge into your very being allows you the opportunity and inclination to share this with others. That is what being a true emissary and teacher means, for as you teach and preach, it sinks into your soul more fully. It is always that way, as you know.

Days will pass quickly for you as you begin to walk the path of life in the light, for everything before you is luminous in its clarity, for no other path will fill you with such joy and happiness. So many people struggle and fight against their own inclinations to follow their God, and this causes unhappiness and despair. You know now that this new way is far more satisfying, for it gives you the strength to choose each moment for your

God-self's glory by doing and saying the right thing. As you get further into this way, you will find it will come naturally to you, and every facet of your life will be transformed. I am with you every moment, my Dear Ones.

Record-breaking heat is about you right now. The humidity contributes to a day of hardship for many and a day to stay indoors for protection. Elderly, children and pets are the most vulnerable and some will die as a result. Of course, air conditioning helps a great deal so it is wise to stay in a safe place to get through this period of high heat and humidity.

A place of protection is also recommended for most who feel secure living amongst loved ones or loving people. Life is best when one stays in a place that feels like home and is comfortable. This is the way it always was for families of the past wherein most people lived their entire lives in one small section of the world protected and content.

Now life is much different for most as the world is the playground and abode for those more adventurous souls. It is not uncommon for children to have many places in which to reside and be schooled. Some adapt very well and become cosmopolitan individuals more open and willing to travel and learn.

Widespread travel even a hundred years ago was not for the common man or woman. It was a choice for some, but they were greatly outnumbered. Planes were not a means of travel, whereas trains and boats were more common. It took many, many days to cross America, much less the planet.

Today many travel extensively and are able to visit many countries in a relatively short time. Some revel in this opportunity and become very transient individuals.

Because this has changed over the years, life now is much quicker and fuller in many respects knowing that people everywhere have common goals, desires and ways is an eye-opener. Some have rituals and local practices that seem odd, but basically all are moving in the same direction. We are placed here to grow, learn & eliminate practices or ideas that are limiting and archaic. Living a full life is really challenging but extremely rewarding. Go this day with these thoughts that ALL are created equal and no one is better than another. I am St. Germain.

Summer is nearly over, and fall is coming soon. The winds are stronger now, and the trees are beginning to shed their leaves. It is a vibrant time wherein all are preparing for the winter and the precipitation it brings. How happy all will be with the pleasant days and cooler nights when sleep is deep, and the mornings are darker allowing more ease of slumber.

It is also a time to reflect on all that has happened and that which will soon appear on the horizon. Reflection time is helpful and brings greater clarity to your mind. If changes need to occur, it is a perfect time to plan, plotting a path to a happier life free of worry about finances and all that this freedom brings. Money is energy that you can use to great advantage so it is wise to mentally and physically draw it to your world.

Be still and hear the voices of your guides and angels for they are near to assist you and bring you to a better way to live. They standby protecting and steering you to greater accomplishments giving insight and greater understanding of your path. Listen for their encouragement, and follow the leadings they set before you for your growth and acceptance of life's bounty.

I am here to lead you and bring you to a new level in your life. I am St. Germain.

CHAPTER TEN

POWER OF PRAYER

This is the day I have made. Rejoice and be glad in it. You need to be joyful in My Presence, for joy is an attribute you sorely need. It will become an integral part of your personality and soul, for joy is an offshoot of the awareness of My Presence within you.

Your soul feels good when you center on me, for it is actually the normal state for you. You bring eternity to your doorstep when you pray these decrees and concentrate on My Presence. The more you put your thoughts on me, the more can I place within you and before you every good thing. You are drawing into your presence those who will be of like mind, and in so doing, your life will have more meaning and depth. Happiness and joy go hand in hand, and you are attracting more happiness.

In your decrees it is good to pray for individuals from time to time who are present in your daily exchanges. It is not that you have to pray for them on a regular basis, but even a prayer or two for these who seem in need will be helpful to put them on the right path. It could be a person who is a clerk in a store, or one you meet and spend a brief time with, but your heart will go out to them, and you can say a decree or two for them. It will help; I assure you.

Now, Dear Ones, go about the tasks at hand this day and come to me for assistance and guidance. I am that I am, your Creator and God.

Ladders function by bringing one to a higher level from which a mission can be accomplished. It can bring one to a higher floor or it can bring a librarian to a higher shelf and on and on for there are many reasons why ladders are used.

A ladder to a higher communion with God is prayer for it turns your inner spirit free to ascend to your Creator-God. He/She revels in your attention and answers your prayers as He/She sees fit. Sometimes the answer is no for that which has been requested is not suitable for your growth. Continue to pray and talk to your Creator for it is really the norm to speak to your parents and He/She is indeed your Parent.

Do not wait for a crisis to speak to God but do so daily to keep that connection alive so that when bad times come, you will be much closer to the answers and help you need.

All who dwell on planet Earth are afforded an opportunity to be close to your Father/Mother God for it is desired and reciprocated. Do you turn away from your earthly parents? Then why would you choose to turn your backs on God? Go back to your child-like ways of praying, anticipating answers in a simple trust. Expect all good to come your way for what you put out, you will get back. If your prayer is for abundance and you truly feel it will come, it will. If you want a companion with whom to share your life, that will happen as well. Your Father/Mother God loves you and wants your happiness. Trust what I say for it is truth. I am your mentor, St. Germain.

Tender roots are set down by plants even in the desert. They tap into the life force that renews them by nourishing them with water and minerals that feed them. And so it is with your needs, Dear Ones. By being grounded in the I am, you, too, are being nourished and strengthened to accomplish the tasks that you face each day with ease and, yea, even with power. Each challenge you face is surrounded by the light that comes from your heart that is filled with the I am, for you have called Him to renew your life. You will be amazed at how smoothly your life will flow, for you are in harmony with all.

The laws of nature are rooted in the I am, and when you call this into your life, you are manifesting this every moment of every day. When you feel out of sorts, dejected, sad, angry, or whatever transitory emotion you are experiencing, then do not dwell in this pattern, but renew yourselves by visualizing the Violet Flame rising through your being, and you will immediately find you are in harmony once more. This victory over feelings will increase each time you are able to consciously return to the I am until you find your emotions and feelings do not waiver, but are constant in love, and peace, and even joy, and then you will be victorious over your feelings, and they will be in check and in God.

Our blessings to you, Dear Children of the Light, for we are with you even now, the Ascended Masters and I, St. Germain.

Tall are the pine trees in the forests, reaching constantly toward Heaven and the light that nourishes them in their regeneration process. Mankind can learn much from the beautiful trees and plants around them, for these flourish in the light and produce abundance in the forms of flowers and fruit. I say to you, Dear Ones, be fruitful. Stay in the light of God and blossom forth that the beauty within may be shown to others. Let your "branches" reach out to touch others that they may be comforted and enlightened. It is necessary for you to show compassion to others, for their immediate needs must be met before they can open their hearts and minds to the Almighty I am.

Speak forth God's truth, but not until you have shown others God's love that dwells within you. You need an infilling of His love daily that you might function in this world and, in fact, flourish as the trees that touch the sunlight above them. You notice they not only reach up to Heaven's light, but they are also embedded in the earth, where they are fed in order to grow.

So it is, Dear Ones, that you need to be grounded by Mother Earth and nourished by the living waters. You are placed here on Earth, Dear Ones, and it is necessary for your growth. Your strength for your physical body comes from the earth beneath you, and it is necessary to realize this for you must have others around you from whom you learn lessons and grow in strength and power to face your daily tasks.

Be still and know the wonders about you. Be joyful that you are alive. Breathe in the oxygen given off by the beautiful trees around you. Send forth the carbon dioxide that supplies them, and you will be in balance with Mother Earth. Find peace and solace in your hearts and in your fellow man as you exchange the wonders of life with others this day.

I am White Buffalo Woman consoling you and comforting you.

The soft beauty of a sunrise dwells in your soul. The dramatic wonder of a sunrise encompasses your life, for the Mighty I am surrounds you and fills your world. Daily meditation brings you into the light of love, and the rest of the day is a celebration in the flow of love and life that dwells within you and moves out to others in concentric circles of light, drawing those you meet into this joyful, wondrous world in which you live and move.

The joy that fills your soul is felt by others, and they are drawn to this. When someone says you are charming, they feel the glorious God-Presence you've allowed to increase in your soul. Be it ever so slight in another, the response is still there. They may never totally understand what it is they respond to within you, but they will indeed react and be blessed in the process. The grace of God can often flow through a person, touching a cord deep within one who is searching, for know this: All God's creatures are searching for unity with the I am.

Prayer and meditation connect you with the Creator as nothing else can. It is a direct line as though you picked up a phone and dialed a number to infinity. The boldness of acting toward God in a connected, prayerful manner is what will strengthen the bond between creature and Creator. Hold tight to this way of life, for the rewards it will bring are boundless and instantaneous. Prayers, Dear Ones, are indeed answered. All God's gifts flow out to those who beseech the Father, for He delights in giving abundantly. It may seem strange to you that the I am is such a loving God, but it is true. He is pure love and therefore gives constantly an unconditional love that overwhelms the recipients. Open your hearts to receive this greatest of all gifts––love. I am your friend and guardian, St. Germain.

Continue to pray, Dear Child, for all you are presently praying for and more. Add your children, the Earth, and its inhabitants, and pray that future events will be softened by renewed faith and love in me. Hard times are ahead, for it is unavoidable. Much damage has been done to Mother Earth, and she needs to restore herself. Much destruction and death are ahead, for in her cleansing, she will indiscriminately cause earthquakes, storms, and water to cleanse herself, and, yes, she will turn herself so that lands will lie dormant underwater to heal themselves, and other lands will rise where there is only ocean now. It is a hard process for all the inhabitants of Earth, but necessary in order to come to a new age and life. Change is necessary for growth always.

Now place your future in My Hands, and I will allow that which is for your good to come into your life. Do not take one step without inquiring of me first. Allow me to lead you step by step just as you led your children when they first began to walk. I am leading you now as you toddle after me. You are still in need of My Careful Guidance and you *will* have it. The future is shining before you as a bright light leading you on. Get involved with people, and your happiness will be that much greater.

A cloud bank appears solid as if you cannot break through it, and yet a plane can move through it, a bird can fly through it, and even man could move through it if he could fly. There are many walls that can be broken down through prayers and decrees. The Berlin Wall was broken down, and its symbol was oppression to the people of that land. Yet communism has been weakened by the prayers of countless people, so it no longer poses a threat to humanity. Walls of all types that separate people can be broken down through prayers. When there is a wall between you and another, just decree for that person, and the wall will eventually crumble, depending upon the intensity of your prayers. Continue to pray for your supposed enemies, for it will break down any and all barriers. With some it will take more time, for they are stubborn and unwavering in their self-aggrandizement or selfishness. People who have low self-esteem find it through putting down others. Of course it is wrong, but you need to understand that they are weak individuals who feed off the strength of others. They feel bigger when they put others down, for they call attention to themselves, but the attention drawn to them is the opposite of what they wish, for others see through them to their weakness, and in fact they are really causing people to look down at them. It is not necessary to enter into arguments with them, for they are masters at arguing, so the best way is to ignore their pettiness and do what you intended to do in the first place—just live the best you can and do what you feel is right. They will expose themselves in their weaknesses, while you maintain your own strength. They know the games of the world, and you are learning the truths of the Spirit. Go in peace this day and continue your walk. I am St. Germain.

Aprons cover a person's clothing thereby keeping them clean and protected, preserving the integrity of the individual's appearance even after a messy job is finished. You, too, have a protective cloak around you, Dear Ones, and it is the light of the Mighty I am. It is important that you pray the decree for yourself at least twice daily, for it will indeed preserve your integrity. The world grows denser as more people succumb to the darkness that surrounds them. Those who sit constantly in front of their televisions are hit with not only the radiation, which weakens their bodies, but more importantly they are bombarded with negativity that drags them down emotionally, thereby reducing the quality of life for them. How sad it is that small children are subjected to this negativity that way, too, for it snuffs out the natural joy of living with which they entered this life. This society is so overcome with negativity that violence is spreading everywhere into the most sacred places—schools, homes, the streets, and, yes, even churches. No place is safe from this darkness that pervades the workplace where so much time is spent by so many.

You, Dear Ones, can change your world, your homes, your workplace, by decreeing, praying for God's light to enter in and take hold of all around you. Remember I have told you the light you call forth by decreeing spreads out 50 feet in all directions. The I am's light is pure crystal white, a gleaming iridescence of such intensity that no darkness can remain in its path. You, Dear Ones, can call forth this apron of light about you each moment of each day, for it remains with you as you walk along the path of integrity and love. I am your friend, Arcturus, and I wish to encourage you to truly live a life of glory in a world so overridden by complacency and darkness. Do not hide this light of the I am, but share it with those around you. They hunger and thirst for nourishment and hope. The I am dwells in all, but it is essential to call the higher realms into your world. Pray, pray, pray each day as often as you can, for balance, and strength, and, yea, protection from negativity.

Heaven and Earth are but a thin veil apart. When your prayers rise up to me, angels carry them up in a steady stream as the flow continues. Pray that My Mighty Presence be revealed to all who hear of me, for I wish you to speak forth of me and My Mighty Violet Flame that heals each one through whom it pours. All manner of healing is needed by My Children of Earth, for such dense darkness exists and, yea, is rampant here on this planet. As the saying goes, "You can cut it with a knife!" It is so dark here from all the negative thoughts, feelings, and expressions that have gone forth for ages. The clearing of the darkness will take mighty work on the part of My Light Workers in the form of teaching, clearing, and praying. It is a gargantuan task that will need the assistance of *all* the Ascended Masters, for the next decade is a very important one because changes will occur that will cause all men to look to sources beyond themselves. A mighty age is coming that will allow light to shine forth on Earth for the first time in thousands of years, for a new golden age will rise from the ashes of destruction mankind will experience. The old must be destroyed before the new can come forth victor at last. It is the reason I am calling you and countless others to assist people in preparing for the times ahead. If I have called you, will I not prepare you? Then open your mind and hearts and let the lessons begin. Today I will continue your healing and instruction through My Servants that you might be just a little freer and ready to climb the mountain toward ascension and freedom. In your climb many of like mind will join you and will find me, their Father-God, ready to receive them and you in My Light and Love. Blessings to you now and forever.

I am that I am.

CHAPTER ELEVEN

NATURE'S TREASURES

The rolling hills and green grass, the babbling stream that leaps and sparkles its way down a course, the magnificent trees that bring life to humanity by just being and emitting oxygen, the puffy clouds above, the velvet beauty of the night sky with its sparkling, diamond-like lights from the cosmos, the rainbow arch that lights the sky with its colorful display, the weaving wheat and corn that flow with the wind's gentle breeze, the peaceful animals that graze on the grass, the little animals that scurry to and fro storing their food for the cold winter ahead——all these wonders of nature comfort you and bring you a touch of the I am. Altogether they compose nature's gifts to the eye of mankind.

The sounds of the world bring harmony to the people of this world who are in touch with life around them. The humming of the bees and birds, the call of the wild animals to one another, the barking of the dog in the distance, or the soft mew of a kitten——be aware of the sounds of nature and life about you. All the senses can be alert and awakened to the treasures of nature's gifts.

To be truly alive, begin to concentrate on breathing deeply *prana*—— life——into your lungs and throughout your body. To be fully alive, fully human, and fully aware is the most wonderful outcome of being in touch with the I am.

When a new life comes into existence, be elated for the promise this life holds to others. When a life flows out of a loved one, be elated, for this, Dear Ones, is part of life, and this soul moves on to new adventures and is awakened to a new existence that brings greater enlightenment.

Accept life as it flows to you for the lessons you are ready to receive. Hold onto love that courses through your being, and then let it pass on to others.

I am White Buffalo Woman encouraging you to live fully in the now.

Raindrops fall to Earth, sometimes gently, sometimes with pelting force, and they join together to form puddles, streams, rivers, seas, and oceans. It is taken for granted by Earth beings, but it is truly a miracle, for water is life to all vegetation, the animals, and the changing patterns of the landscape. This can be likened to the manna from Heaven that descended to the children of Israel in the desert.

You are always more aware of God's presence when you go out into the wilderness. You are able to appreciate more the beauty of nature's bountiful gifts to mankind. The greens of Earth are restful to your eyes, the earth colors are warming to your soul, and the expanse of blue sky and white clouds expand your being and soul. It is a renewing experience for you to sit in the stillness and concentrate on your I am Presence, for that is when you hear that still, small voice within. It is calling you to even deeper communion with your I am, for it is in stillness and aloneness that you can more easily go inside to feel your Presence and know the joy of discovery of the gems of truth, light, and love that dwell inside and permeate your very roots and soul that is indeed divine. Such a revelation was known only by mystics and chosen ones at one time in man's development, but now, Dear Ones, it is not so exclusive but can be shared with many, many souls about you. Continue to pray, and the miracles you witness around you will be spectacular. I am White Buffalo Woman, and I send you the feminine life force from Cathedral Rock in waves, undulating waves of nourishment to your soul.

Flowers are perfect examples of the love of God manifest on this plane. They have beautiful little faces upturned in worship of the I am. By just being, they give praise. They emit a sweet fragrance that attracts insects and honey bees to them to perpetuate their way of life. Humans enjoy these little harbingers of God's love by smelling them, enjoying their beauty, and capturing this beauty in photographs or paintings. Even though their lives are brief, they have brought glory to creation and their Creator, as well. That is what you must do. By being and turning your faces up to the I am for sustenance and supply, you, too, bring glory to the Creator-God. You are the highest form of creation on this planet, and by just being you, too, bring praise to the I am. Think of the beauty of this world, and give attention to it that you might learn how you can come to your highest power. It, Dear Ones, is to just "be" and have a pure heart that will emit a sweet fragrance to those around you who will be drawn to the beauty that dwells within you––the I am.

Feel the love that fills your soul, for when you bring the Violet Flame through you, you are bringing up pure love, which stays embedded in your heart and soul and fills your being with a wondrous feeling that no other source can give you. You are blessed, Dear Children, to have the love of God running through you consciously, for it allows the pure love to be accepted into your lives to be used to move through this plane more easily and happily. Continue these decrees, and you will be amazed at how sweet life can be, for you will be awake and aware of how wondrous life truly is.

I am your friend, Arcturus. Go in love and peace this day and all to follow.

Animals of all types are gifts to mankind for they provide help, affection, food and pleasure to many who avail themselves of these wondrous creatures. They were created to assist men in his lengthy journey on earth.

In return it is man's duty to treat these special emissaries of God's love with respect, kindness and reciprocal love. It is not right to abuse, neglect or destroy their lives for they do have feelings and are susceptible to disease and mistreatment.

How can you not love a tiny puppy or kitten? Any baby animal carries God's imprint and comes into the world wanting comfort, care and love. Sometimes they are abused and mistreated right away, not by their mother but by humans whose hearts are dark for they are destructive to all that are near, including these innocent pets.

As the animals mature they are often not "cute" anymore and so are set free to forage for food, shelter and attention. There are so many animals in this position and often are put to sleep because there are no caretakers for them. They sense when it is time to die and hold back physically and emotionally. It is so sad to see these poor creatures pass so quickly and prematurely. It is hard to believe that some are so immune to this that they would take part as "executioners" for want of a better description of the people in charge of killing them.

This is not what we ask of you. It is best to nurture animals and close pets for your reward is immediate from the animals and from angels who hover nearby. Continue to treat all animals with kindness and send love to the squirrels, butterflies and birds of the air for they receive it and sense you are kind. They will always be your adversary, here and the hereafter.

Go in peace today and give love to all animals, large and small. I am your friend, White Buffalo Woman.

The earth is a magnificent testimony to God for it was created to assist mankind, to bring blessings and to be a reminder that something much greater than "self" created all we see and use our senses to enjoy. The shimmering clouds, the mighty mountains resplendent in beauty beyond imagining, the vast expanse of oceans and seas, the towering trees who give us life .... all these are reminders of God's splendor on Earth.

The teeming life that makes Earth home contributes to the wonder of this awesome gift. There are reminders everywhere you go and in all you see about you daily. Open your eyes and heart to the great variety of colors and visuals about you and your soul will rejoice every second of life on this great planet, Earth.

Concentrate on beauty and your soul will be revived, and you will once again feel the wonder and exuberance you once experienced in childhood. Do not lose sight of whence you came for there are reminders at every turn in the lonely road of life. You can find commonality with all creatures, great and small, and this loneliness will vanish in an instant. You were meant to shine with life oozing from every cell of your being. When you realize how blessed you truly are, you will sigh in contentment and peace will be with you evermore. I am White Buffalo Woman who truly appreciates the beauty of creation.

High above the mountain tops clouds gather and descend covering these purple peaks of wonder. Snow settles on the mountain and glistens in the sunlight. It is a magical land that draws many to its top for the beauty is unsurpassed anywhere on earth. The magnet it is is tangible to adventurous souls who relish the moment that they stand tall on a precipice of ice crystals and snow. It is a sight they live for and cherish forever.

You, dear ones, can reach the top by living in the arms of angels and beings of light for they surround you at all times as you walk this earth of splendor. How can you doubt that you are special in the eyes of your Creator for He/She sees the beauty in your soul and amplifies that quality with His presence. You are so special that angels minister to you and hover about you caring for your every need. If each person on earth saw the beauty that flows from their heart, the seat of their soul, they would fall on their knees in worship of the Divine and never want to rise.

You are human as God intended so enjoy all that comes your way and those you meet along the path. Bask in the sunshine, dance in the spring rain and allow the snowflakes of winter to touch your cheek and gather at your feet. Sing, dance and walk in joy for you are blessed and cared for in a special way by those you allow into your space. It is comforting to have friends and family who adore you and wish to walk for a time beside you. What more can you ask for if you are loved and cherished by many? There will be times when this is not so. Bless those who defile you and walk away for it is not to your benefit to remain in their presence. Holiness does not come overnight but is realized slowly as a bud opening to dew drops and blossoming into a radiant flower. You will blossom too and spread joy throughout the land.

I am your very special guide, White Buffalo Woman.

Green, a very soothing color, represents many facets of life and living. Green was used liberally by Father/Mother God, the Creator of all that is. Meadows, trees and all the greenery of earth is visible constantly to all. It is very calming and, as such, people are able to function in a way they could not without that healing color.

Green also represents everyday life as well for "green-backs" stand for the money we use daily to live life effectively. In recent years it has diminished in value so that many more citizens are struggling daily.

The elementals care for the varying facets of life; the trees, bushes, plants and all life in the forests and woods. They do a fine job that has not been recognized by most. Their duties are immense, and they take them seriously. They fear for the earth because there is a lack of water that feeds the plants, and so they urge man in subtle ways to conserve and stand up for regulations regarding water. It is not something for us to fear but concern would be a better way to live. When there are opportunities to speak out or physically conserve this most necessary commodity of earth, then do so until you are heard.

We encourage all light-workers to be aware of the danger imposed by not respecting the earth and its wonderful abundance. The bounty of earth is appreciated by all for they partake of these gifts daily. The prayer, "Give us our daily bread," is significant for it prays for supply and God listens and gives abundantly to those who pray and honor the gifts and the giver of gifts.

Go this day in peace and try to be aware of the earth about you. Spend time among the verdant trees and honor them with your care when necessary. I am White Buffalo Woman, lover of Earth and its goodness.

The red planet is being explored now as never before. Much money and time has been spent to catapult the curiosity-seeker into space and ultimately to its destination. It is a feat of gigantic proportions intended to explore another planet. Much will be learned to benefit mankind and its approach to discover the solar system and its planets. Much more will be learned in the future, and it will blow minds in the process. The surface has been scratched, and there is much undiscovered that will give an idea of creation's wonders.

Daily you walk this planet appreciating its vastness and familiarity. It is comforting to experience the status quo as you know it. More "secrets" will be unfolding in the near future about this planet and others as well. There is a commonality and mystery involved as well. Scientists explore the unknown while most men merely wonder accepting the reality of terra firma called Earth.

There will be vast knowledge coming to substantiate and upset man's thinking. As always, things are not as they seem on many fronts. There are intelligent beings on other planets in other galaxies that are far more advanced. They can help this planet succeed as never before in its explorations. They visit this planet often for they too are doing their own investigations.

You have been fortunate to see first hand a vehicle from space and know they are indeed real. Someday soon all will "know" that extra-terrestrials do in fact exist. Peaceful interchange will happen at some point, and your lives will change drastically.

I am your friend and teacher, St. Germain. (August, 1990 three of us saw a UPO fly over our house in Sedona, Arizona under the Airport Mesa at 11 PM.)

Melons will soon grow and give their sweet, succulent flavors to millions who will enjoy them at their peak of flavor. Summertime gives many opportunities to enjoy the warmth and the crops produced for all to enjoy. It is a time when neighbors greet one another and spend time jointly enjoying the sunshine and soft breezes. The rustle of the leaves overhead are hypnotic and restful to those sitting beneath these beautiful trees. Life is pleasant to enjoy after a long winter and spring of cold, snow and rain.

Take this opportunity to be out and about soaking up the pleasant days and nights. It is a time to celebrate life and exchange time with family, friends and neighbors.

Visiting the ocean is a special occasion for many who wonder at its vastness, enjoying the gentle winds that blow across the waves to kiss cheeks and move on. Boating and sailing are enjoyed by many for it brings great pleasure to skip across the water in a vessel of choice.

The long, warm (and sometimes hot!) summer allows many to breathe slowly and relax. People need down time and summer affords that opportunity.

Coming home after a long day of work, the earth gives off its coolness for the evening wherein one can eat a leisurely meal with family enjoying this peaceful time.

Surround yourself with this carefree time and blend your life with others to make peace with Nature and its frivolous ways for it can be sunny one day and pelting rain with high winds the next. Tornadoes and hurricanes are common across the land breaking up the peaceful summer bringing terror and death to some who are in the storm's path.

And so it goes, the balance of Nature and Life. Take in the good and release its opposite and you will find it easy to cope with all conditions of weather.

Balance is the key to all for it represents Life in its varied forms. Peace be with you now and always. I am your friend and proponent, Arcturus.

Chapter Twelve

BE HAPPY!

Joy is a wondrous state of being. Without joy, life is stagnant, for no life is felt or appreciated. Joy is a state in which our hearts sing. It is a tune that all can follow, for it uplifts all who are in the presence of the Joyous One. God gives joy to those who center on Him. How can one not be in a state of joy in His presence, for He is pure love? Oblivion to all around, but God, is a gift to those who persevere in getting to know Him better. If you do not seek Him in prayer and meditation, how can you expect to know Him? Do you not spend time in the presence of the one with whom you have fallen in love? Then does it not follow that to know God better, you must come into His presence often? Do you truly understand that He dwells within you and that you need only give Him your attention? Be still and know Him, for His relationship is the key to all you need forever. He stands waiting for you to open the door of your heart to Him. You will never be disappointed, for His love is the only treasure that goes on through all eternity. Treasures of the Earth *will* be left behind you when you leave this life. Everything you own will go to someone else after you pass on, but God's love will be with you always. Think on this today, for it will be the key that opens the doors of Heaven and brings Heaven to

Earth. My love to you, and may your days be filled with joy and love. I am St. Germain.

Love is the answer to a happier, more fulfilling life, one in which each day is a new adventure, and everything seems to be in focus and magnified. Peace and love go hand in hand, for a heart filled with love is indeed at peace. The journey through life is meant to be fun-filled, happy, and glorious no matter what is going on around you. Negativity and turmoil need not be part of your life. Commune with nature and be grounded that all may flow easily for you. Do you see little animals sitting in despair or wandering around saying, "Woe is me!" They move through life effortlessly and trust that all will come to them, and it does. They chirp, sing, and make their own sounds of pleasure and happiness. They are positive and free to live joyfully. If you would live with the confidence that God, your Father, will always provide for you, you, too, would be able to sing, hum, and make sounds of a positive nature, not letting negativity ever settle into your world. Put aside all negative thoughts, for they are certain to contribute to your demise in more ways than physical. Do you not enjoy being with someone who is happy, positive, and fun-loving? Then become that type person yourself, and you will attract others of like mind into your life. "Smile and the world smiles with you. Be sad or cry and you cry alone." It is true; is it not? Think back and you will know you repulsed people when you were in anger, sadness, depression, and the like. Smile, be enthusiastic, and be happy, and you will find many friends with whom to share your joy. Go in peace this day and find joy along the way. I am Arcturus, your friend and fellow traveler.

Enthusiasm is a powerful tool to bring wonders to your door. Life is exciting when you come into each day with a renewed outlook, an expectation that clears the path before you so that beautiful things happen to give your life more meaning. Butterflies, hummingbirds, and little creatures of the Earth will come to you, for they love to spread joy to humans and be appreciated. These colorful little gifts will be drawn to you, for they sense you will receive them with open arms and hearts. You will be like a magnet attracting gifts of love from your Creator.

To be like a little child receiving from your God is how you can live if you choose to do so. It is a conscious choice for life that is manifest in such a way that all you meet will be better for having been in your presence. To be light in spirit, anticipating, expecting, is the most wonderful way to live. To be able to laugh and giggle is so healing for your soul and body. Accept all that comes your way, and learn to roll on the waves, bobbing and playing as you move along. To be as a little child comes from knowing who you are and what your life purpose is, for then can you release your cares to your God and begin to enjoy each day knowing you are provided for and loved.

Life brings good, and there are times that sadness comes, too. Remember to stay in balance, and do not get so caught up with what appears not to be good. There is a time when you will not feel joy inside, but if you can feel at peace and remain in peace, soon the joy will return. I am your friend Arcturus. I had to learn this, and it was not easy for me. I am here to help you so that it *will* be easier for you. Blessings to you this day.

CHAPTER THIRTEEN

VISUALIZATION

Violet is a soothing color, which man instinctively gravitates towards in this time of great change. It is the essence of the Divine and shrouds one in its protective cloak of pure love. It brings great comfort and solace to those in need. This is why you see more people using this color at this time. The pure Violet Flame consumes the darkness that still clings to your aura and obliterates it forever. Visualize the Violet Flame not only filling your being but surrounding your body, for then it can work to purify you all the while it is protecting you.

I wish to tell you more about visualization. It is important that you visualize all that you feel will make your life more comfortable. The more specifically you can visualize, the faster and more complete will be the effects of your visualizations. I do not speak of dreams, Dear Children. I speak of special visualizations that are given power to be manifest in your lives. This is a powerful form of prayer. If you visualize a new home, and see it with a clear picture of its detail, and hold that idea in your mind as you pray, it will be drawn to your life. Begin to do this, and you will see I speak truth. Also visualize whatever will make your life more complete, and it too will come to you. There is no need for you to want for anything as a child of the Divine, for you can indeed draw to you whatever you wish. The key to realization of your wants and needs is to see it clearly coming to you, and this alone will set into motion the vibrations that will attract that which you desire. Your mind is a powerful tool, which is used so little, and yet the potential for achievement is right there within you. Give this a test for minor desires, *but* be specific that you might measure the results. Then you will have confidence to move on to greater manifestations of the Divine. I am Arcturus and bid you joy and happiness.

In the center of the sun dwells the I am. In the very depths of the sea dwells the I am, for the I am is the Creator-God and lives everywhere and in all persons, places, creatures, and things. It is so difficult to realize that the I am is everywhere, and, Dear Ones, He dwells within you. Try to understand this, for it is important to know this and truly accept it, for it is one step toward your ascension, a very important step.

The birds that soar in the skies near you contain the I am. The fox that darts across the fields is filled with the I am. All creatures, large and small, contain the light of the I am. To some are granted the privilege of seeing this light that is the Divine. I say to you, you, too, can picture this light flowing through everything about you by concentrating on the I am and seeing this in your mind's eye. This visualization will enable you to step toward actualization in you. I mean that you truly accept and know that God is all and in all. Open your eyes, see the beauty of the I am all around you, and begin to appreciate these simple truths that will change your lives forever. When you start to change, you begin to move into a new life that will be more satisfying than anything you ever dreamed possible before your awakening. We bless you always. I am St. Germain, your mentor.

CHAPTER FOURTEEN

COLORS

Green light is healing to your soul, as it is to your body. The color green is a color used for healing. When people wear green and use green in their living space, it is because they instinctively feel the need for healing. It is a color used by the Creator a great deal, for every shade is seen in the trees, bushes, and luxurious grass you trod upon. Breathe in the green light for healing of your body and your soul, for it truly works as a balm, a soothing ointment for your being. Each color of the rainbow has a special power or healing, and humans glory in the rainbow, for it is truly a promise of new life. Each color of the spectrum has power to heal one aspect of man's soul and each part of his body, as well, to be more youthful. Breathe in the colors your instincts tell you your body, soul, and spirit need for deeper, more lasting healing.

The I am has given man the ability to be whole. By filling yourselves with the rainbow light of the I am in your prayers and meditation, you feel the effects of this wondrous healing light. The Presence fills you with an intensive light that truly satisfies your every need. Aging speeds up when the light is not recognized or neglected, for just as man needs food and water, he also needs to open to the rainbow light of the I am. Visualize the colors your higher self tells you, you need, and breathe them in deeply several times, holding your breath and the thoughts of the color. Color therapy is very beneficial to you, as well, whenever you are able to avail yourselves of this gift.

Be mindful, Dear Ones, of the wondrous effects of color upon the soul, and gather about yourselves the colors you feel will be helpful to you.

Think of the blazing red that bathes one, for it is a powerful energy booster, the strength that can be used when needed. Embrace the oranges and yellows, for they boost your joy and allow your spirit to soar and bubble with love. Think of the green, so calming and healing, that was used so liberally by the Creator. Surrounding yourself with hues of green is far more soothing than 1,000 massages or mineral baths. Blue is the color that arrests anxiety and brings God's caress to your being. When vibrant, it charges your soul with electric energy to perform tasks of gargantuan proportions. The indigo and violet are the colors of this new age of enlightenment. They are the royal colors heretofore reserved for kings and queens. Now is the time to fill yourself with the violet flame colors of purification and enlightenment, for now is the time you need protection from the dark forces that oppose the light. All these colors are found in the pure white light of God, His gifts to the artist, and appreciators, as well, for He clothes the Earth in the majesty of His light and love and allows these kaleidoscopic colors to flow through all. When you pray and meditate, you act as a magnet, drawing these colors to your aura, which filters them as they pass into your inner being to do their work of cleansing, healing, and purifying, and then flow out to others as they come into your presence. Think on these things, for these truths will make you more aware that you are a vehicle of God's love, light, and very presence. I am your guide and mentor, St. Germain.

Green is a calming, healing color, which you need around you in your daily life. You notice how much God used it on the Earth, for He intended it to be healing for His creations. The softness of the sky, with its blues, pinks, oranges, opalescents, and yellows, is a wonderful contrast for man to enjoy. And so you have the healing Earth colors—browns and greens in all shades—and you also have interspersed colors of the flowers that bring such happy feelings to the viewer. Color is very important in the lives of all individuals, for it sets the tone of life. When you choose colors to wear, it is usually because you need them to replenish lost energies through the intensity of living in such a dense existence. Your chakra colors blend to give your aura its light. When green is predominant, your body and soul are undergoing healing. When blue is predominant, your body is resting and replenishing itself or balancing itself. Oranges and reds indicate a person is in anger or rage and seething inside. Yellow can be either sickness or high energy and is God's light, for it is so close to white. A greenish or brownish yellow shows sickness in the body, whereas a bright, sunlight yellow shows balance and closeness to God in the person's soul. The white light depicted in paintings of saints is truly real, for this is what one sees around those who have reached holy enlightenment and closeness with their God Presence, allowing that Presence to shine forth. When violet light is seen in a person's aura, it shows that the radiance and infilling of God's presence is taking place in the individual. It shows an openness to receive the Divine in a more tangible way. It was a color for royalty because it allowed the king or queen access to God's assistance in ruling wisely and with clear direction for the ruler's subjects. It also cleared away selfishness, greed, and the like for the ruler's mind, although this was not always true.

And so, Dear Ones, color is very important in the lives of so many people. Go in peace this day knowing we are here to help you. I am St. Germain, your friend and guardian.

Pink is a soft, pleasing color, which represents love. It is the color of life––pink checks, blush of pink, the pink glow of a sunrise that holds the promise of newness, the pink body of an infant newly alive with the gift of life in its heart. To be young, pull in the pink light that will revitalize your cells, giving you a more youthful appearance. Allow the life-giving force of pink to surround you, comfort you, and refresh you.

The colors are a gift to you from the Almighty One. Each one has a special glow that brings healing, joy, happiness, and much, much more. Colors enhance your life by bringing their vitality into your living space that you will feel the beauty and be at peace. Have you given thought at all to how important color is in your existence? Do so, Dear Ones, for you will be led to those colors you need to help you grow, be healed, be strengthened, be wealthier, and be more loving. I promise you that we will show you those you need, for you will draw them to your life simply by choosing them for your clothing and décor. Have you not noticed how you are drawn to articles of clothing in your closet? It is often a feeling you have for a certain color, and so you choose that blouse, shirt, skirt, or pants, for it feels right to you. Know that we are often directing your choices by enlivening a color so that you will select it and gain assistance from it.

In closing let us remind you that your growth is always happening through large and small occurrences or those people you allow to come into your life, even for a brief time. Every day is bursting with promise of new opportunities to grow and change into a more loving, aware, alive individual. Be happy, Dear Ones, in this knowledge, for we are here helping you all the time. May God's light shine more brightly in your soul because of the beautiful colors, the varied people and opportunities that flow by you each day. I am St. Germain filling your mind and heart with wonder, and joy, and peace if you will only open up to our gifts.

Black is a color that is actually all colors, for it absorbs all other colors. The connotation of black has been twisted and abused throughout the centuries to represent evil or the dark side of man's nature, and yet it is really no worse than any other color per se. It is what it is, a unique color that contains all colors. Humans have misconstrued the true meaning of many truths, and so people go through life believing half-truths and sometimes untruths. You are not meant to believe everything others tell you. Test all that is given to you, for there will be times when your spirit will instruct you otherwise. Allow your guardians and higher self to lead you and guide you. Your feelings often show you the way to go, and believe, and with whom to associate and share time and space. True, you must love the Presence, the I am, in all you meet, *but* that is not to say that you must spend valuable God-given time with each one. There are those who will help you to grow, and there are others who will hold you back, as well. Once again your feelings and intuition (which is really your God-self helping you) will show you the ones you should be with, for you will feel comfortable with them, and their behavior will be worthy of your time and attention. It is better to have fewer good friends to share with than to have many with whom you can have surface relationships. This is not for you, Dear Ones, for you are not politicians or such who rely on surface friendships to achieve goals. Share your time with others of like mind and inclination, and you will grow and find happiness. Love of self first allows you the privilege of sharing love with others in a meaningful way. I am St. Germain showing you a better way in which to live. How glorious life is when you love and feel loved as well.

CHAPTER FIFTEEN

LESSONS

Time

Time is all in all. What you think is today was tomorrow, the future, just yesterday. The past, future, and present all blend together, for there is truly no such thing as time to the Almighty I am. When you feel other presences, as you do in this place (near Bell Rock), it is because there were many others here through the centuries of time, as you perceive it. You feel especially the Indians who trod these paths many times. There were indeed battles and skirmishes between the red and white men not far from here at all. People were born here and died here, as well, for that is the balance of life. People stood here with great plans in their hearts only to have their hearts stilled but moments later. People have always felt the energy here, so life went on all around this place. Close your eyes, and in your mind's eye you will see these people and feel their presence, as well. Whenever you are near a place (a battlefield, for instance) where others died, the memories of that event linger sometimes forever. You also feel the sadness and even despair of those left behind. This sadness also takes hold of a place and is felt by those coming into the area and lingering a while. What I am saying is true of many, many places on this planet Earth, for people here do not accept death as a part of life. They see it as a bad thing and not as a freeing of a soul to move on to other lessons. This is why, when you see past lives, you often see the death point of your previous personages. It was a traumatic experience, and so it remains attached to your memory. Begin to see death as a wonderful transition time for your friends, loved ones, and self, and you will not fear it any longer. I am St. Germain and have taken this opportunity to explain your feelings when you are in a place such as this. Enjoy the beautiful sunshine and this moment of your life——live in the now.

Wholeness

Mountains shrouded in mist are mysterious, but it is merely an illusion, for soon the vapors rise, and the mountains are once again normal in appearance. People now are shrouded in illness, but it is real and not getting any clearer. It is time to clear their bodies, for the times ahead will necessitate their becoming well again. There will be opportunities to come more fully into God's light, and therein you will find healing. There are forces upon this planet working against mankind, and many will succumb to their destructive energies, for they weaken the immune system, opening man up to the viruses and germs rampant in this society. Have you not noticed that more people are sick, and others are not feeling well, dragging through each day with little energy left to truly enjoy life? Then you know what I say is true. You, Dear Ones, are being called to wholeness in your physical bodies as well as your spiritual selves. You will be shown the way to wholeness through those who come into your lives. Be open to this cleansing, for we will ask much of you in the not too distant future. You have two choices, Dear Ones. One will lead you to good health, and the other will lead you down the path of destruction, to be bound to karma for many, many more lifetimes. The first one is the better one, of course, for it will lead you to a fuller life in preparation for your ascension, returning to the Great Love, the Almighty I am. We will be here to assist you in choosing life. I am Arcturus, your friend and companion of the light.

Cathedral Rock, Sedona, AZ

Serene is the world about you, for this is a blessed spot in all the world. The energy here gives you strength and peace all at the same time. The little winged creatures have been curious about you and fly about you to determine what your place is here. To speak again of the energy that comes from the Earth at this place, I wish to say it is truly an energy that is emitted from the Earth, which attracts to it those who are seeking knowledge of the I am and how each one fits into His plan. Each must find answers for him/herself. The energy here allows Sedona to be a spiritual place, which even the Indians recognized. When you live here, you are being bombarded with energy at all times, and this speeds up your process of growth and change. It is not always easy to withstand this constant renewal process, but in the end, if you can allow it to happen, you will be a newer creature and child of the light than what you were when you arrived here in Sedona many years ago. Anodes deal with electricity, and so Sedona is well named, for it is a form of electricity/energy that comes from within the Earth. All holy places on Earth have this same energy, and so many spiritual beings are drawn to them. You could say this is a holy city, but, remember this, all who dwell here are not of the light, and so you must use discrimination in choosing those with whom you wish to associate and be with on a daily basis.

Enjoy the days you have left here, for we will guide you away from Sedona before too long. Trust that we will bring you to a place where you can grow more in ways you haven't thought about as yet. Do not dwell on this idea, but know it will come about gracefully, for when the time is right, you will seek a new dwelling place. I am St. Germain, and I wish to surround you with peace and love of the I am this day.

(Anodes is Sedona backwards!)

Humility

The lesson for today is humility, for this simple manifestation is one of the most difficult to maintain by messengers of the Word of God. I call you all to walk humbly with your God, for in this way you set aside your egos in order to be pure channels of the Almighty I am. When your ego and self-aggrandizement come forth, they overpower the light of God, diminishing it to a dim light covered with gauze, preventing it from shining forth and lighting the path of newcomers to the love of God. It is not part of the plan of spreading the Word, and so I caution you. Allow yourself to be quiet, and attentive, and humble before the Almighty, and you will win souls one after another after another by your loving, caring, pure self, who knows where the power comes from and who gives the glory to God alone.

Humility is the pivotal force that allows more knowledge to come forth to be given to the masses that sorely need to hear about the Almighty I am Presence. Always check yourselves and help one another to remain in humility and love.

Continue your way this day surrounded by light and love that can satisfy your deep longings for unity with God and therefore with those of like mind around you. Be at peace. I am St. Germain, your teacher and leader in the love of God.

Forgiveness

Continue to walk in My Way. Continue to look only to me. Trust that I have your welfare at heart. My Plan for you is not to destroy you but to remake you into a useable servant. Allow me to refresh you and comfort you. It is My Love that will renew you. Join the angels in praising me. Praise will release a dynamo of power that will restore fortunes and resolve differences. The fortunes are the love of brothers and sisters for you and your love for them. That is what lasting fortune is all about. My Love is renewing and restoring what has been lost through pride and, yes, even arrogance. My Ways must by rights be sought, and in the finding, you will have peace, and love, and joy. Forgive and release your resentments, and I will be free to work out all difficulties. Whatsoever you bind on Earth is bound in Heaven, and so it cannot work freely. Release resentments before they become bitterness. Forgive and release, so I can work in him/her, too. Try to understand, for I will give you what you lack so that it will become pure love, My Love for him/her. I am working this out My Way, and it will be done. Trust me and relax.

Diet

Caramels and other candies are sweet to the taste but cause many problems in the body after being consumed. Discernment in your diet is very important, for many foods are destructive, while others are empty of nutrition. These foods hold back your spirituality, Dear Ones, for they make your body denser and less able to be filled with God's divine light. We ask you to monitor habits. Stay away from sugar in all its forms. Coffee, tea, alcohol, and other stimulants are also detrimental to your health. The pure foods or "live" foods are best for your nourishment, such as fruits, vegetables, herbs and growing plants, grains, seeds, nuts, and even some flowers. The Earth provides bountifully of the foods you require for good health and spiritual growth. Be more mindful of what you put into your bodies in order to be lighter beings filled with God's light and love.

We ask you to change your daily living in order to grow and absorb the light energy that we send to you and with which we surround you.

Sadly only a fraction of God's light can fill you, Dear Ones, for you are not sustaining a proper diet. Think of food as fuel. To be so attached to sweets and stimulants will bog you down and attach you to the Earth and not to Heaven. Open more fully to the radiant light of the I am by controlling your eating habits. We will assist you in your attempts to eat purely by increasing your discernment of what is best for your body, mind, and soul. As the days move by, you will see more clearly what you must eat and drink and how you must live to be healthier and more open vessels for God's light and love. You have been chosen to spread God's Word and need to be cleansed, healthy beings in order to be more effective emissaries of the Divine. I am St. Germain admonishing and encouraging you in a very important area of life.

Trust

Love My Gifts as you love the Giver of All Gifts, me—your Lord and Savior. Trust me to lead you one step at a time. You were not created to leap about like a gazelle but to walk, putting one foot before the other. Walk after me. Let me lead you along the path of My Spirit into a glory land of bright lights, sunshine, warmth, and love.

I, your Lord, am waiting for you when you falter. I will continue to guide you, but you must continue to trust My Leadings. Trust is the beginning of deep love. The more you trust, the deeper you can come into My Presence. You will not be disappointed, although at times it will seem as though I have departed from you. I will not, *cannot* leave your side. You are in me, and I am in you. We are inseparable. Trust me, My Child.

Call to Service

So, My Child, I am working out all your problems and your problem areas. You will be totally renewed to face the tasks I will set before you. I called you and you answered My Call (just as Matthew). You were a servant to the ways of the world, but now you are My Servant, and I will use you even this day.

Some days you will be lonely and feel rejected. Remember I, too, was rejected. People will sense that you are not of the world. Some will be repulsed by this, for neither can they accept nor understand this. But others that I have chosen and are being drawn closer to me will recognize your otherworldliness and will be drawn to you—–the me in you. I am about a mighty work in you, and, yes, even in your whole family. I will allow miracles to befall you. I will go before you daily clearing the path, preparing hearts to respond to you. Speak boldly for me, and I will uphold you, and encourage you, and even give you the words to speak.

Live In Harmony

A box is many-sided, and yet it forms one unit and its function is useful to mankind. And so are each of you many-sided but very useful to the I am, for He can fill you to overflowing with His divine light and love, and you can then be utilized by Him. Always remember you are unique in all the world, your talents being very different from the one next to you. Because you are different from others, there are tasks that only you can accomplish, and in so doing another part of God's plan is fulfilled. Each being on this planet has talents, and that is why each is part of the whole, for only that person can do a job uniquely in his/her own manner. It is amazing when you consider this, for the plan is so gargantuan that only the Godhead sees the entire blueprint for the accomplishment of the beautiful existence He calls us all to enjoy. Each is asked to contribute his/her share to the all. By cooperating with others in your daily lives, you are putting into action the marvelous talents you have been given. Live in harmony,

Dear Ones, for that is essential to the entire goal of your lives. Selfishness, conceit, deceit, and the like hold back each child of God from reaching his/her full potential. These must be relinquished in order to live as God intended. Allow the Violet Flame to flow through you, eliminating these flaws and imperfections as they fall away, making way for the beauty and strengths to be increased and expanded to fill the space in your "box." I am Arcturus and give you encouragement this day to fulfill the divine plan for your soul.

Life's School

A squirrel is an animal that is often put down in our society because it acts quickly and runs about a great deal. It is only acting as nature dictates, for it is a busy little fellow constantly searching for food and storing it, knowing instinctively that a day is coming when times will be harsh and difficult. Humans could learn much from this industrious little creature, for it holds many keys to success. Hard work and concentration on inner strength will bring many a person through difficult times. Learn from the behavior of others, including God's wondrous little creatures. Each moment of life is an opportunity for learning and growth. Mistakes are great teachers––it is true––but understand that observing the patterns of life others set, as well as instinctive actions of animals, can give us very great lessons from which to learn.

Life is a wonderful school if we can take the lessons presented to us in many, many ways. Brief encounters with others can often redirect our lives in ways we had not dreamed possible. Enter each day with the thought that opening your minds, hearts, and sometimes souls to people you meet will push you to greater limits and test your belief system that it might be ingrained more deeply in your mind and heart.

Trust the I am will lead you to those who will help you all the while you are helping them. There are no accidents, Dear Ones, but merely lessons and times of growth or opportunities for the same. Go in peace this day with the knowledge fixed in your minds that the I am is in charge of your learning, as you have allowed this to happen. I am St. Germain encouraging you to be open, be wise, and be happy in the world of the I am.

Duality

The cutting edge of a knife is sharp. It can be used for good by cutting vegetables or performing tasks wherein a knife is needed. It can also be used destructively to wantonly damage another's possessions or to snuff out the life of a person or animal. It has a duality that can work for good or bad, depending on the intent of the owner.

All life has duality. It can be good, whereby one lives in the light with love the modus operandi, or it can be in darkness, wherein one lives his/her life out of feelings of anger or despair. One who acts this way can make life miserable for many people and, in fact, all who come by him/her. It is as if one drops a pebble in a still pool, for the ripples go out in all directions and touch every leaf that floats in the water or boat that is near. When we act in love, this also flows out to others in ripples, soothing and touching lives of those receiving this love, as well as those they meet, and so on, like dominoes touching other dominoes on and on. All feelings have the same effect, for they touch many persons through the one we display—anger, or disdain, or whatever.

When one in despair acts out their anger toward someone by overt acts, countless lives are affected and changed forever. Oklahoma City is a perfect example of the results of senseless acts of violence upsetting a whole nation and beyond. It is not in God's plan that man treats his fellow man this way. The karma created by these few is far-reaching and will take many, many lifetimes to overcome in these individuals. Remember this, however, to put things in perspective; the ones exploded chose to do so to complete karma of their own. Death of the body is so feared in this society, but remember this: it is not how you die that counts, but how you live your lives that is important.

Start now, this instant, to appreciate life and those you live beside daily. Live each day as if it were your last, and see how this will change your life completely. I am Arcturus bidding you peace, love, light, and joy in all you do and say.

Vigilance

Trains are no longer a main method of travel since planes are much faster. Other modes of transportation are also not the efficient way to transport individuals. And so new ways of all sorts of everyday comforts are constantly changing to improve life. At times it seems we are being plowed over by new inventions, and life is thrown into top speed leaving many behind, befuddled and confused.

Life is much easier in many ways thanks to ingenious inventions and advanced ways to do almost everything. There are, however, some things that are not improved; such as, trust, honesty and believing in a man's word. A handshake was once considered a done deal in business. Now that is not the case and one must be vigilant that they are not being scammed or robbed. The internet opens the doors and windows to schemers who take advantage of many individuals who used a credit card or gave too much information online. People have been wiped out financially by robbers who leave no trace to their whereabouts. It is sad to know that so many are duped and left penniless.

How does one cope in a world so corrupt? The best way is to be cautious dealing with only those you know are trustworthy. In doing business you must be vigilant and keep accurate and lengthy records. It is a sad statement on society that principles have gone by the wayside leaving uncertainty in its place.

We urge you to be in tune with your guides and listen carefully to your intuition and gut-level feelings for they are merely urgings for you to follow in order to be safe. I am Arcturus encouraging you to be safe and secure in your lives.

Seasons

Corn is being harvested as are so many wonderful vegetables and fruits at this time of year. The nights are getting cooler while daily animals scurry to and fro stocking up for harsh weather that will soon settle on the earth. These are cycles of life with which we are all very familiar. It is a pleasant season wherein people are enlivened by the comfortable, active days and pleasant nights for sleep. It is time to sit in the sunshine and welcome the warm touch of the sun's rays and the pleasing scents of fall that flow to us with the gentle breezes.

Creeping in with each passing day are harsher winds and the chill that means winter is approaching rapidly as we all brace for the stinging bite of frost and snowfall we have put behind us these many, cheerful spring and summer days.

All these changes keep us in tune with life passages from youth to middle age to our long-awaited final days of wisdom and knowledge of life's messages and secrets. So many in this society stave off old age as long as possible for youth is adored and worshipped. Yet the final stage of life is most freeing, and we are comfortable with whom we have become. All the veneer of youth wherein we are exploring our selves is behind us. "Youth is wasted on the young," can seem true to us as we venture into the final stages of life. Our bodies do not function as easily as they did when we were young and living in our declining bodies is more difficult. It is a wondrous preparation time for the future life beyond this transitory life on Earth. The life ahead is feared, but we still have a curiosity about the Transition called Death.

And so life moves on from childhood to adulthood to old age, and with it we grow and mature and find our stride. It is best to appreciate every stage of living with no regrets for the mistakes or tragedies we endured. They are best left in the past while movement toward the future with all its adventures and promise of renewed life just as the seasons of Earth coincide with life.

I am White Buffalo Woman bringing messages of hope to all.

Country

Men and women fought and died to keep this country free. Their intent was pure. Unfortunately there are people who want to enslave the citizens of this country using many means to suppress growth. Stand up to them, and do not give away your right to life, liberty and happiness. You were not created to be slaves. You were created to shine brightly because the Creator chose to imbue life within you. Hold your heads up high and fight for love and the right way to treat one another.

No one is better than another. All were created to be equal. Money and wealth is not meant to be your god for it did not breathe life into your soul. It squeezes the life out of its recipient, especially when it came as a result of running rough-shod over many people. Stop this madness before it sends its roots deeper into the earth. It is incidious and harmful to many, many children of the Divine. We are <u>all</u> children of the Divine and, as such, have a responsibility to help one another achieve a better way of life which has its inception in love.

I am your proponent of working to overturn these incidious acts perpetrated against the populace of this great and glorious land, America. I am St. Germain.

Parenting

Mothers are very special to us for they sacrificed much to bring us to adulthood where we will be set free to live our lives. The lessons we learned from our parents live on in us to be responsible citizens of the Universe or not if our lessons were of a lower dimension. We are responsible for our actions, and then we pass these lessons on to our children and so on it goes from generation to generation.

Life perpetuates the good and the bad for that is how it flows. When we teach our children wrong lessons, society reaps the negative. If we try to instill noble virtues in our children, then the benefits are perpetuated and many people are affected for the good. It is so important that parents understand the huge responsibilities they accept when they bring children into the world. Unfortunately, these lessons of parenting are often overlooked by society and young people in particular do not know how to parent correctly. Not all people should venture into this important area of life for they cannot take care of themselves much less another person. Prisons are filled with the product of this incorrect upbringing where virtue was not understood nor passed on to their children. It is sad indeed that so many are harmed by the lack of love and discipline in their childhood. Sometimes rebellion is the reason for their incarceration for they were not loved or taught properly. Rehabilitation is not the norm in our society so prisons' doors revolve for many who return to an empty life which is often dangerous as well.

This was not God's intent that so many lives are wasted. These men and women who are banned from society lead lives that are unfulfilling, restless and produce angry individuals who lash out at anyone in their path. There are millions of people living this life set so far from life as you know it. How sad.

Dear ones, lessons start at birth and continue throughout life. The early lessons learned are the ones that send us forth into life. Society cannot continue to overlook these unfortunate people. Pray that these lost souls find peace and solace. I am your mentor, St. Germain.

Compromise

Not all people think as you do, and it is necessary for you to understand that it is all right. Voice your opinion and state your side and then back off and be silent. In this world there are many who are not flexible and hold firmly to their ideologies thus causing problems and disrupting many lives. Politicians at this time are most guilty and will not allow compromise which is and has always been a way to solutions and outcomes that benefit the majority. Since so many refuse to compromise, your government is at a stalemate and needs fresh air to blow aside the obstacles. You will see that in your elections for most people are tired of the do-nothing representatives who take up space and refuse to reach any agreement but their radical policies. You will soon see a result of their obstinate, unwavering ways for it has not gone unnoticed by your citizens who will rebel through the ballot-box. This will free your leaders to get the job done of straightening out this sad state of affairs. So much unfairness has caused strife and hardship for the main body of your citizens. It is time for change and a trip back to equality and sensible solutions to so many of the problems your country faces. Hold tight and await an outcome that brings newness and liberty for all. I am your confidant and supporter, St. Germain.

Democracy

Along the highways and byways of this great land, you see beauty and sometimes the not-so-beautiful. This is a land of great heart and opportunity, and it is imperative that this idea of democracy must be protected. ALL are created equal in the eyes of God. Those who view themselves as wealthy and above everyone else have no idea that all could be stripped from them in a heartbeat knocking them down to join the rest of humanity. Death and disaster have no concern for whether one is wealthy or poor. It is very disconcerting to see that many people feel they are on a higher level than others. There are times when someone who is very poor is what your churches call a saint for their heart is pure and their love for all is very great.

The Word of God states that you must treat all equally and accept all into your space and heart for there may be angels among those you embrace as brothers. Go this day with the idea firmly fixed in your mind that ALL are connected and equal. I am your friend and ally, St. Germain

Chapter Sixteen

WAKE UP!

The earth is in turmoil and at jeopardy for I have given man free will. It is in a precipitous position, hanging on for dear life, and man goes about his way with nary a thought of how his greed affects everything. All are connected and if one drops a stone into a pond, the ripples flow out to every bit of bank surrounding it. Consider this earth as the pond and see the repercussions of the vile acts perpetrated on innocent peoples everywhere. Only it isn't just one stone being dropped but thousands upon thousands of evil thoughts and actions against the populace at large. No wonder people are so insecure. They sense that Evil personified is set to destroy all within its path leaving a barren, desolate planet to flow with the wind because no one will be left to navigate it to safety. These are dire times and that could be the result if people of heart, connected to God, do not awaken and fight for freedom and the salvation of Planet Earth. Read this and weep, dear ones, for that will be the end result if people of love do not unite and fight for justice, fight for peace and stamp out hate and injustice that rears its ugly head all around. I beg you to rise up and stem the tide of evil attempting to snuff out good and love from the planet.

The planet has suffered enough. It is time to reverse this horrendous manner of treating the earth and its inhabitants. Pray, love and live in harmony with all about you, and pray mankind will wake up so that all will live in peace and harmony never before seen on this wondrous planet, Earth. I am your Mother/Father God begging you to wake up.

Swirling clouds of discord assemble all around this great nation. How sad to see so many split factions throughout this hallowed land. It is time for unity of purpose not based on selfish goals but born from Love.

This "building" will crumble if the splits continue for if the foundation of a structure is weakened, it will not stand. The foundation of which I speak is written down in the Constitution which was Divinely inspired and given to men of substance and principle who knew that any disharmony would be detrimental to the Nation they conceived and planned.

There are still many living here who desire unity and justice for all, not just a few. Your citizens must stand up for the concepts set forth in the infancy of this great land and that was, of course, liberty and justice for all. Too many are struggling and do not feel they are a part of the initial plan. They feel downtrodden and put-upon by those at the top. They suffer at the hands of the evil few who steer the leaders astray. If this continues to blossom, there will be revolts and once again Civil War will be upon the United States. This is <u>not</u> God's intent but He/She allows free will and, if the people continue to "sleep," it will not be what the majority want.

This nation is at a turning point. If those whose main purpose is greed have their way, the results will be disastrous. Pray and pray more that this does not come to fruition. Anger goes hand in hand with greed for those who wish to step on all who need assistance or turn a deaf ear to the poor and weak of America's citizens. Unless <u>all</u> are treated with love and caring, the Nation will not stand but will be weakened by the corruption within.

It is time to stand for what is right! All men and women deserve liberty and justice. I am St. Germain standing in the wings ready to assist any and all who wish to fight for the freedoms set down in writing by your forefathers.

I, Arcturus, bring you greetings from on high and bid you pleasant days and peaceful nights for time is of the essence and the future is in your hands, dear children of the Light.

You have been forewarned that the future struggle of good and evil is at hand. Never before has the outcome been so dire and important. Peoples of Earth who desire peace, unity and love <u>must</u> unite and fight for those freedoms. It is not a time to sit back and allow others to overcome your way of life. Harken to my words for they will be strong and direct for all must listen and heed God's words of wisdom and love. Wisdom and calm are the anecdotes to all sorts of assaults, verbal or physical. How can an evildoer attack when one (or a group) is not retaliating? Instead it is best to stay calm and use communication to offset the anger and hate that confronts one. Be still and hear the voice of reason. Stop and call for God's help to resist and overcome.

The future is at hand. Will you allow others the opportunities to degrade and demolish your way of life? Then if you want to keep your freedoms, you must listen and act. Do you want war? Would you prefer peace? Ah. If you desire love and peace to reign, you must step out of your comfort zone and speak out and stand up for justice. Will you allow greed to rule? Then stop and think of how you can overcome the vast amounts of money being spent by greedy men who wish to take away all your freedoms, reducing your personhood to a dot. You are not created to be weak but to be strong in your convictions. Too many sit back eating and drinking themselves into oblivion while the world crumbles about them. They soak up the lies and untruths spewed at them on television shows and give their rights up to others whose only concern is wealth, riches and power. How sad it is to see the downfall of man! If you think it is only Africa or China or some other far-off land, you are wrong! It is a moment that is worldwide for there is a group who controls far more than you can even imagine. It has been underground for many generations and is rearing its ugly head in the open far more than man has ever seen. You think you have free speech in this country? You are wrong! The news is controlled by a few and is not the truth. Remnants of the truth come out here and there but is squelched immediately. People of integrity are rebuked, put down and, as often as possible, stopped. That, dear ones, is what is happening openly and defiantly and not in a covert manner. Do you not see? Then it is time to act. Before revolt is necessary, you must stand together to stem the tide of greed, avarice, prejudice, hate and lies spoken out by so many angry men and women. Compromise is not part of their bag of tricks. Love is not part of their mentality, but empty promises are presented as truth but is so far afield you won't recognize the outcomes of their intentions for they are not for the good of mankind, the 99% as you call it. Instead they want to throw mankind to the wind stripping every good thing from their tables. It is time to act for we are our brother's keepers and unity is the only remedy to stop these indiscretions and blatant acts of injustice to all except the very rich who will become much richer as a result of the plans being implemented at this time. You are being tested and unfortunately it's been going on for a long time. They perceive the stagnant nature of most people and feel it is time to do their dirty deeds to the populace. Wake up! Wake up! Wake up! It is time to act!

Now is the time for rejuvenation and growth. You are being pulled aside to allow us to strengthen you in every way––physically, emotionally, and spiritually––for you have many tasks to perform for us in the not-too-distant future. As you can see by the news, this is a world that is tottering on the brink of disaster, and we, the Ascended Masters, are using everything at our disposal and within our realm of power to dissipate the evil tendencies of man. Do not be disturbed by what you hear, for we are counteracting all that would destroy this planet and the lives of so many who are truly walking in the light of the Almighty One of Eternity. Know this, for I speak truth, and remember it always: There are very few people on this planet who intend evil to the masses due to the darkness they hold in their hearts and the greed that has totally overtaken them. Most men do not understand them, for they are so far off base that even these few do not know how far afield they have wandered; therefore, they cover their avarice by proclaiming they act for the good of all under their command. What is even sadder is that they truly believe they are following the correct path. War is all they understand, for in their hearts they justify their acts and intensions and cover them with a semblance of their love for mankind and God (or Allah, which is their belief).

We are working very hard to stop these blatant acts of aggression by opening hearts and showing many that they must act and stand up for the beliefs that fill most hearts on this planet. These demonstrations will continue and increase to such an incredible degree that world leaders will have to act differently.

Now, Dear Child of God, go in peace for the most exciting, rewarding, and fulfilling part of this life on Earth you are experiencing stands beckoning before you. Our love and guidance is always at your disposal. Avail yourself of that at all times, and time will flow so quickly that you will soon be standing next to us.

Be happy, Child, and smile for then all the same will flow into your life. I am Christ, Sananda, Jesus, the Holy One of Heaven, who has been with you always. Thank you for loving me and know it is returned always!

Acute times call for action from all who dwell in the Light for drastic measures are in order to quell the evil attempting to ascend the world stage. There are a few who make Mother Earth their home only to strip her of her treasures leaving behind devastation, pollution and dwindling animals who are so close to God's Kingdom. There are ways these evil-doers can be stopped, but it takes attention and hard work by those who rebel against the unholy acts committed on Mother Earth and her progeny in the form of vegetation and precious animals of all forms, including mankind.

You, dear ones, can do your part by signing petitions, marching in protest and, most of all, becoming well-informed and voting against those who wish to suppress the many to make the few wealthier. It is not right to stand by and allow this to happen for it is your duty to stand against those whose hearts have turned to stone, living their lives without compassion or caring for their fellow-man.

Women have always been suppressed but not the manner in which many would increase it to squelch women's power that they inheritantly fear. Be strong and fight against this openly vicious attack on women's rights even in countries that are supposedly more advanced. Americans, in particular, need to awaken to what is happening all around them from men who live in fear and choose to bring others down to their level.

It is time to open your eyes and "see" what is occurring at every turn in the road. Take off your blinders and stand tall against your oppressors. If they have their way, you will be enslaved and broken. Is that what you want? Then fight for your rights with every fiber of your being that the evil-doers do not win their sick arguments and only caring for the wealthy while stepping on the rest of their fellow-citizens.

Wake up! It's time to take action. We are here to assist and defend you. You need to ask, and we will be beside you in an instant. I am your defender, Arcturus.

The Fourth of July will be here soon. It celebrates your country's birth at a time when peoples of this land were divided – some remaining loyalists and the rest staunch supporters of the infant country.

And so you are at a crossroads once more in this wondrous country of the United States of America. There are those who wish to move forward assisting the poorest and most vulnerable of your citizens with respect and love the foundation. But there are many whose main care is self and their greed will go to great extents to snuff out compassion, to concentrate on selfish desires of power, money and fame. Money is no object in this fight of freedom vs overt slavery to the wealthy few who really do control men, money and the future. If too many lay dormant not caring what transpires, the outcome will be disastrous and your country will move back into the dark ages where women are defiled and racism is rampant.

Is this what you want for your future? Then it is high time you wake up and protest the attacks on your way of life for, dear ones, it is in danger.

The poor will be in dire poverty not seen ever in this great land. Your "middle class" will join the ranks of the poor and down-trodden while the very few at the top will be wealthier than ever before. You will be back to the feudal era when the entire populace genuflected to the few lords at the top.

Is that what you want for the land of the free, a time when freedom will be squelched to appease the very wealthy who will control mankind as never before in the history of the world? It is time to stand up and speak out protesting against the foolhardy plan to dominate all who dwell beneath this fifty-starred flag. Revolts will rise up as never before when the citizens wake up to what is really transpiring, and you very foundations will be shaken to the core. These few who intend injustice and slavery for the masses will awaken a sleepy giant, a mass of people who will fight to the death for their freedom and very lives.

Wake up, Dear Ones, and raise your fist in protest to what is happening for you will regret your complacency and inaction if you do not stand up for justice and the American way.

I am St. Germain with strong warnings of dire circumstances that could be deadly to many, many souls.

The die is cast for America. Cleansing will be necessary in order to purify her for the future age of wisdom, light, freedom, and love. The land is entering a time of testing and tribulation, wherein all *must* pay attention to what is happening. There will be much destruction of property and possessions, and many will pass through the veil to a new life with memories of what has come about. They will have to select a new life on this planet or another incarnation elsewhere to allow themselves the opportunity to come to enlightenment. This is God's law at this time. All must choose to grow and change or to be in situations where this is more plausible.

Continue to concentrate on the I am, for you will go through this time knowing what is happening and why. We have not said this will be an easy time for anyone, for much will be different. Each must make choices that will allow for the future of his/her soul growth. Moving through this time of trial will change each one forever. Growth can be rapid, so rapid that the very dimension in which you now live will not be the same. A time warp will occur to catapult you into a much higher dimension. It will confound you for a time, but the adjustment will come, and you will feel much more whole than you've ever felt. Great joy will fill your soul and being, for at no other time in history has this opportunity been in existence. The total condition of life about you will expand in the twinkling of an eye. Hold fast to this promise of new life, for it will happen as I have said. I am Arcturus and will be here to help you.

The birds of the air float, dip, dive, and trust that the air will uphold them and bring them safely down to Earth. You, Children of the Light, also trust that the I am will uplift you and allow you to float and even dip and dive if you choose to do so. You see how much easier it is to float on the knowledge that the I am protects, uplifts, and sustains you at all times? Rest easily on the Presence, knowing full well you can trust the God within to uphold you and ever be your haven of protection.

The next several years will see profound change, and man will put down his guns and be concerned with his own safety and salvation. He will begin to find in his heart some of the strong emotions and start to feel again. Emotions that have been driven way down will bubble up in many hearts that have been hardened by false philosophies and beliefs. Terrorism has been the result of these callous beliefs. Man will be so frightened and shaken by the events of nature that he will once again seek his Creator for assistance.

Consider this a glorious time, for the end result will usher in a time of great peace, joy, and renewal. I am your protector, St. Germain.

Justice will cover the land like a warm blanket. It is time for people to withstand the onslaught of greed-ridden individuals whose main concern is self. People are waking up all across this sacred land moving forth the agenda of righteousness. Men and women are seeking fairness and the American way for all who dwell beneath the fifty-star flag.

The inception of this country many decades ago was dedicated to the preservation of justice and fairness for all. Through the course of the past two centuries it has wandered off the path of freedom for all. Hatred, prejudice and greed have clouded the original intent of our forefathers so that now there is poverty, sickness and injustice for too many who are crying out for help. These are our brothers and sisters. But for the grace of God, each of us could be in the same circumstances.

It is time that Americans help their own citizens achieve the American Dream which is shrinking rapidly for far too many people. Stop this insanity from continuing by every means possible. Wars in far-off lands drain the United States leaving less for its citizens. Do you understand why war is backed by so many? It is due to greed once again for military contracts for goods are lining the pockets of many who cry out for wars to continue their avarice and ill-conceived plans.

It is time to put down guns and pick up the reigns to justice for all peoples. Concentrate on the problems within the borders of this great land, and goals will be attained one by one until life is sweet for all once more.

I am your compadre, St. Germain

Greetings! I am your mentor and friend, St. Germain. I have come to share my thoughts with you this day. Evil is all about this wondrous planet, Earth. It is sad, but true. Overcoming this evil is a huge task and will require the efforts of many, many light workers and people of heart whose main goal is to live at peace with all mankind. God's mighty right arm is needed to give impetus to this path to wholeness for all. The struggles of poverty and wrong thinking are at the basis of this movement called terrorism. People have been duped into perceiving wrong outcomes for dastardly acts of violence as the norm. It is against what they perceive as "evil" for their goals are not pure but warped and unconscionable. They treat their women as though they are slaves and pawns on a board. Equality is not part of their up-bringing or basic thought patterns. (There are remnants of this in most societies on Earth, including America the beautiful!)

How do we deal with these wrong-doers?

That is the problem for it can take generations to weed out their misconceptions of right and wrong. Jailing, torture or the like is not the way either for it only increases their mindset on the side of death and destruction to infidels. How wrong they are and, remember this, there are scores of men who think this way. Eruptions of reactions to misguided remarks and actions by "infidels" always brings retribution. It is seen over and over and over again all across this globe.

Respect for their beliefs will help but, unfortunately, that is a lone solution not big enough to quell the fires of hatred dispensed by them. America was awakened quickly on a beautiful, sunny morning in September to the reality of devastation and destruction of lives and property deemed a threat to your way of life in America. Retaliation has taken many paths and wars to protect this way of life often too sadly at the cost of young, vibrant men and women whose suffering is given to save millions who adhere to life, liberty and the pursuit of happiness. Now even that is dwindling at the hands of greedy men who are set on destroying the government and, consequently, the peoples of this blessed land. They need to be stopped. This will only happen when enough citizens wake up and realize they are meant to be responsible instead of pawning that privilege to others who often have only selfish goals as their modus operandi. It may be too late to stop this tide of greed sweeping your country. People will once again be torn from their complacency as 9/11. Then there will be revolt, and it will not be pleasant.

Pray, dear children of the light, that this is not the outcome. Pray that enough will wake up and actively pursue justice for all. It is not too late, but will take a new way of thinking that ALL are created equal in the eyes of God. Start now by treating all well with whom you exchange your lives on a daily basis. Start with your family and go out to friends and finally to strangers. A smile is so far greater than a frown. I bid you adieu for now and will return with more directions as time passes.

Pink is soothing, gentle & reviving for those blessed to allow this soft color to surround them permeating their very soul. Pink needs to envelop the world for it sorely needs to embrace the love that this wondrous color inspires. Pulsating, tangible love is the balm for Earth's wounds inflicted upon the peoples of Earth by those whose only goal is power, greed and self-worship. They will meet karma head-on for the sins they have committed on others whose only goal is to live in peace and harmony. These desires have been pulled from them in the affects of war waged against innocents.

Woe the men who perpetrate these odious acts of violence! Lives are being snuffed out by those who desire to rule their part of the world and beyond. War is not the answer to any question. How do those who desire peace deal with these evil men? There are ways to cut off their paths through peaceful means. Stop the flow of goods to them until they beg for help. Try peaceful negotiations when they are ready to listen. To retaliate is <u>not</u> the key to victory for it only continues to cause pain and grief for those in its path. Fighting fire with gasoline gives disastrous results and the fire magnifies by hundreds. It is far better to use intelligent tactics that will bring the same result. Your leaders are in conflict with this because so many live in the past only seeing war and its financial gain as a way "out." Those who desire other means must speak loudly stirring citizens to act with thought and peace as their goal. The struggle is intense and stubbornness is not free to open doors to mediation and peaceful tactics. Ego is the main obstacle, but pride always leads to a fall.

I admonish those who stand in the way to Peace. Light workers arise and stamp out ignorance. It is time to stand up for truth and justice that all may live in peace and recognize a higher power at work in their lives. Pray for the time is short. Tempers flare where there ought to be love and reconciliation. Pray that eyes are opened to what is happening that all will join forces to fight for the salvation of Mother Earth and its inhabitants.

I am that I am, your Father/Mother God. I feel your pain, peoples of Earth, and I am here to help when you come to Me, your loving Creator.

The oceans seem vast to peoples of Earth. They are much more connected than you think. Pollution of all sorts is being dumped into the oceans all over the globe and is compromising the purity of the seas. Just as on land, many creatures of the deep are suffering and dying. It is a sad situation for all creatures, big and small. They are being inflicted with diseases and poisons that take hold of their systems slowly reducing their immunity opening them up to toxins that strip their bodies of life.

When will man wake up to how his neglect and greed is stopping growth of many animals, fish and birds of the air? It is time to wake up and smell the ocean's breeze and know even it is not safe from predators in the form of fishermen who use huge nets capturing good fish they want and dolphins and such who are wantonly killed in the process. Once again the greed of mankind is at the base of these operations for it is not enough to gather food but to gather huge quantities of fish that cannot reproduce replenishing the ocean. It is time to regulate what these few are doing for soon the oceans will be empty and that food source gone forever.

We stand by and watch what is happening to all of the earth. It is sad to see such destruction inflicted on the creatures of earth whose only goal is to live to aid mankind and not to lend themselves to greed's way.

Pray, dear ones, that strong people will come forth to protest what is destroying Mother Earth's abundance given to man by God to assist in his/her journey on earth.

I am your friend, St. Germain, feeling distressed for the ocean's beautiful bounty.

Strawberries, blueberries, grapes, cherries are now in season from various sections of the country. How fortunate you are to have fresh produce available to you. Throughout history it was not as accessible and people longed for the blessed growing season when fruits and vegetables were readily abundant and appreciated. Times have changed and wherein one is able to have more food available to them, it is also true that the closeness to neighbors and families has dwindled because so many people are more transient and apt to move long distances several times in a lifetime. It gives one pause to determine if this is the best way to live or was it better to have constants of family and friends in one's life throughout its days.

The world has shrunk through wider and quicker communication so that "news" encompasses the entire planet. Struggles throughout the world make headlines everywhere. It can be overwhelming to hear and see injustice and inequities that exist in far off lands.

Be attentive, dear ones, for the same could happen in your beloved homeland. Be vigilant and, if need be, be active in protesting injustice and overpowering of all sorts perpetrated on the masses. I can't say more explicitly that people must be cautious and aware of what is happening all about them. If you are attentive now and demand your civil and human rights, you will live in peace and harmony for a long time.

There are those, however, who seek to destroy any semblance of fairness and assistance to the common man. To them the common man is as dirt under their feet. Their prejudice, avarice and greed overshadows any degree of kindness and compassion they may have had in their youth. Their conscience is hardened as steel and they only care about their wealth and how to acquire more by breaking the backs of thousands in achieving their goal of absolute power and control.

It is time to "see," really "see," what is happening and use all means to stop this onslaught of the few who are promoting their agenda of total dictatorship. If you think it is not possible to have that happen, think again!

I urge you to wake up and spread the word to all who will listen that Hard Times are at your doorstep if you do nothing allowing the greed of a few (the 1%) to take over this blessed land called America.

How can I be more direct? I say to you <u>wake up</u> and start spreading the word that all peoples must be aware of the dangers lurking around the corner.

I bid you God-speed in accomplishing the tasks set before you. I am your guardian and mentor, St. Germain.

Light is filtering through the denseness of earth's atmosphere and flowing down to all at this time. This is the anniversary of Harmonic Convergence which you were fortunate to witness in Sedona long ago. That was a turning point for this planet wherein God's light spread over all who were willing to accept it into their lives. Now there are many who are allowing the same light times ten to penetrate all beneath it. It will be another important event and turning point when many light workers focus on accepting and increasing the light as it happens, and all will benefit.

Once more man has choices to continue down a rock strewn path to destruction or to take the higher road to peace, prosperity and love. It is man's choice and we, The Ascended Masters, are directing many who will speak out swaying the populace toward Light, love and blessed peace.

When a large percentage of the populace honor our Creator and send love out to the planet, it swings the whole to a greater connection to God, thus fulfilling a promise of life to all who desire it. That is not to say that struggles will ensue, and the few will fight back to overtake the good being brought in. The remnants of the old paradigm is still pushing for the lead. As long as enough realize this and fight back, the war will be won fight by fight.

When athletes are in a game, they play hard right down to the last moment in order to win. That, dear ones, it what we ask of you. Fight to the finish and bring home the gold. Might does not always mean right. In fact, it is often farthest from the truth. Defeat comes when the participants doze off and do not fight for every inch until the end is in sight. That is where earth members are right now, and it's a mighty fight for good over evil. We will stand by and coach you to the goal of an outstanding win. I am your coach and defender, St. Germain.

Greetings from the Ascended Masters and me, St. Germain. I wish to inform you of many items today. Victory is the final goal for Light workers everywhere to pass along words of wisdom, truth and console is the main goal for many of these blessed souls. Now, I ask you to step further into the frey and stir the hearts of individuals who live in darkness, not knowing that God dwells within each person on this planet, including these as well.

What is the most effective way to pass along these words of solace? Your job is to move in love and act out of the same toward all you encounter. It is the most effective way to reach your fellow travelers on the road to eternity. How did you first awaken to the message? Didn't you follow the leadings of just people who spread their love and words of encouragement? It captivated you and you were able to release cares, woes and burdens to your personal God dwelling within. Then, you recall, your eyes were opened, scales were removed and you were able to "see" God in all you viewed. Nature became more alive and beautiful to you. Your family was more dear than ever and your step was lighter and more defined by you heart which was full to overflowing.

Now, I beg you to do the same for others. Love them with God's love, and spread that love freely. Renew your vows to be pure of heart in your dealings with others for the world does not know this type person very often.

People are tangled in webs they chose over the freedom that comes with communing with Nature therefore the Creator of that magnificence all about them. It is time to wake up and be alive. Go this day and spread God's love to all you encounter. I am here beside you assisting you in that task.

Questions: What can we do to redirect the course back to the basics of love, respect and justice for the peoples of Earth? It seems a gargantuan task so where do we start?

The answer is in your heart for therein you will find God's love to redirect the energies of evil you view all about you and beyond. Prayer is helpful because who can resist the pleas and cries of a child one loves? I long to have my created ones live in peace and love with one another! I sent each child to its mother from a place of love, peace and harmony. Have you ever seen a small child frowning and lashing out at everyone and everything? No, instead you see little smiles, cooing and trust in their eyes. Yes, at times it is lost because their new lives are not amenable to comfort, food, love and all the sustenance to give life to these new-born infants. Ordinarily the child feels love, comfort, warmth and nourishment from its mother and family. Then a child can grow easily in love and feels secure, comforted and protected from what seems to the infant, a huge world.

When you see infants, children and people starving because of their cruel leadership, it touches your heart and you feel pain for them. And yet the mothers still try to nourish their emaciated children giving comfort but little food. It is such a travesty! It is such a horror to see! My heart breaks for these who will soon join me on the other side of the veil.

But for grace and love, all could be as these wandering in a vast, dry land. Peoples of earth must wake up for it could spread world-wide and leave total devastation in its path. I admonish you to spread this word, jolting people out of their complacency. Now is not the time for platitudes. NOW is the time for action! Do not turn aside from those in need knowing full well that all are inches away from the same. These are hard times and are meant to turn people away from their wicked ways back to Me, your God. I admonish you all to get on your knees and pray for all in need, including yourself and your family. Recognize me and I will run to meet you where you are for I love all my beautiful children.

At one time in history, I lashed out at the wickedness of some men causing floods and blazing fires of destruction. Yet man continued his wayward path to his own destruction. Now, I only wish to reach out in love and spread my wings of protection to all on Earth. I wish my children to be happy, safe, loved, nourished and comfortable with all who come their way. I will bring peace BUT you must reach out to receive the good I have in store for you. My love is with you now and forever. I am that I am.

Gentle breezes touch one, and it feels comforting and calming. As the winds increase there is a feeling of uneasiness that envelops a person and calm is taken over by its opposite. Then when you are facing the intense winds of a heavy storm, one takes cover and is very uncomfortable until the wind subsides. Gale-force winds are terrifying to the individuals caught without cover and protection, and a desire to be sheltered and protected is foremost in the mind of these unfortunate caught in its heavy crosswinds. The storm finally passes and the aftermath of destruction left in its path is a reminder of the terror felt by all who were in the storm. Tornadoes being the most unpredictable, bring terror and often death to those caught in its path.

Now we are feeling the winds of unrest caused by those who choose to rule over the masses stripping them of their rights and comforts of protection monitarily and socially. As the winds intensify, many will rise up to fight the storms of greed thwarted upon the masses who will rebel against oppression. It is inevitable that people will finally wake up to the evil intents of those who have amassed fortunes and power over the majority. The struggle will be intense and, at times, violent, but might will bring right to the world once more. When the dust of revolution settles, people will fully awake never to allow suppression to darken their lives again. Then will the Golden Age of peace emerge victorious over evil-doers whose main goal is greed and power. The times ahead will be tumultuous but what rises from the dust will be the Phoenix of Peace.

I am your defender and protector, St. Germain.

The time is coming, Dear Ones, when your trust in the I am will carry you through to victory, for much suffering will be around you. You are being trained to move through these times with ease, for the knowledge that all will come to the perfection of God's plan for this Earth and its renewal will be before you always. Tempering is always a trying event for each and every person, but when it is the entire population, it is a harrowing experience, which will be tolerable as long as you remain in the Presence. You will be taken care of in ways that will astound you on one hand and comfort you on the other. Unity of purpose is necessary to bring you through these hard times that are ahead. We do not want to alarm you but to help you understand that it is what must occur for mankind to turn away from destructive ways for themselves and the Earth. They must turn to the I am for their salvation and sanity, for all will seem strange and chaotic. Always know this: It is necessary to come to a world of peace, and love, and change. The New Age of Renewal is before you.

I am Arcturus, and I bring you comfort and love from the Ascended Masters, your protectors and caretakers.

The jungle is more exposed now than it ever was before. Many animals who called it home are no longer safe from encroaching invaders who wish to strip the jungle and become wealthy. This, more than any other single factor, will upset the balance of nature, causing severe repercussions. Weather patterns will be changing more and more. Clouds will form and heavy rains, which once hovered above the rain forests, will extend out and begin to cause torrential rains elsewhere, causing flooding and destruction of all in its path. What was once desert will change to vegetation, and what was covered with vegetation will eventually turn to desert. It is true that cycles are constantly evolving, *but* man has caused this new change, not Mother Nature. She is merely responding to what has been set into motion.

I am your friend Arcturus. Be at peace this day knowing your I am Presence is at the very core of your being, filling you with the sweetness that can never be consumed or obliterated.

Comments from the Author:

The messages in this book were given to me over a forty-five year period. I actually received the messages in Chapter Sixteen six years ago in the summer of 2012. Many of the messages throughout the book were given to me for a prayer group who gathered once a week to pray for friends, enemies, healings and America.

It is my wish that you meditate on these messages from Father/Mother God, Jesus and several Ascended Masters; especially St. Germain, Lord Arcturus, and White Buffalo Woman. Each has a special energy and presence when giving me these messages, though I do not actually "see" them.

Ultimately my desire is that you are encouraged, enlightened, comforted and inspired by the lessons sent to you though me. May God's blessing fill your hearts to overflowing so that you can be drawn closer to the Spiritual way of living.

We arc all human as intended by God, so we do not always follow the path of Love and Righteousness. Keep praying for yourself, loved ones, enemies and the blessed land of America.

Sincerely, Judith Beals

Judith A. Beals

Books referred to in the messages:

Unveiled Mysteries by Godfre Ray King

The Magic Presence by Godfre Ray King

Ascended Master Discourses by the Ascended Masters

"Violet Consuming Decree" (see next page)

Violet Flame Decree

Beloved Mighty I Am Presence, blaze up through me (or person's name) now, your Mighty Violet, Consuming Flame! The purifying power of Divine Love, in its most powerful, dynamic activity! Consume, cause, affect, record and memorize forever all human concepts, desires, and feeling in my (or person's name) being and world, and every mistake for which my (or their) outer self is responsible! Replace it with the Ascended Masters' electronic substance of light, love, purity and perfection and hold your Dominion within me (or person's name) forever!

Almighty I Am! Almighty I Am!
Almighty I Am!

Printed in the United States
By Bookmasters